Endorsements

"I felt so trapped." Years later, with breathtaking generosity, Georgia Morris gently examines young love, mental illness, and her harrowing first marriage. Sporadic delight rides shotgun with havoc. Yet her spirit remains so vibrant, so earnest, we marvel: even madness fails to extinguish her inner light. Retold with the warm, confiding candor of a friend and interspersed with hindsight and Scripture, Morris also gifts us with an overview of schizophrenia. To anyone enduring similar darkness, and to all who love them: draw near. Morris holds out a hand as well as a lantern.

—Laurie Klein, author of *House of 49 Doors: Entries in a Life (2024)* and the classic praise song "I Love You, Lord"

Unfailing Love is a window into the life of a beautiful soul who overcame rape, abandonment, and the terror of marrying a man who was diagnosed schizophrenic.

As Georgia pulls open the curtains and shines the light of God's grace on these deeply personal stories, you see how she walked through these valleys and found healing and new beginnings.

"Don't be afraid, I've redeemed you. I've called your name. You're mine. When you're in over your head, I'll be there with you. When you're in rough waters, you will not go down. When you're between a rock and a hard place, it won't be a dead end— Because I am God, your personal God, The Holy of Israel, your Savior" (Isaiah 43:2 MSG).

—Cecille Russell, founder of Wednesday Warriors Prayer Group and Seattle Is Alive

A Beacon of Hope and Healing

As a pastor deeply committed to the spiritual well-being and soul care of others, I wholeheartedly endorse *Unfailing Love*. Georgia Morris has authored a powerful testament to the redemptive grace of Jesus Christ that serves as a lifeline for anyone ensnared by darkness, heartbreak, and despair—especially those who love and care for people with schizophrenia.

Throughout *Unfailing Love*, Georgia shares very personal insights into how she, through the loving guidance of the Holy Spirit, navigates a labyrinth of shame, abuse, and the suffocating grip of a schizophrenic spouse. Through story upon story, we witness the miraculous truth that God's ever-present love recreates, restores, and redeems.

Georgia's vulnerability and candor are a balm for wounded hearts, and her story is a beacon of hope for those who feel trapped in their own personal prisons … or held captive by the behavior of others. For those who ache for a new beginning, for those who long to break free from the shackles of abuse, Georgia's story offers the promise of new beginnings.

May this book find its way into the hands of those who need it most. May it be a compass guiding them toward the freedom-giving, life-saving grace of Jesus Christ and His everlasting and unfailing love.

—***Kevin Vander Weide,*** pastor of Care Ministries,
Timberlake Church, Redmond, WA

For those struggling with a loved one enduring mental illness, there is hope! In her new book, *Unfailing Love*, Georgia Morris guides and inspires her readers to look to Jesus as their help. Her personal narrative is honest, sometimes raw, and compelling.

Aid your journey to forgiveness and healing by absorbing this story, and allow Georgia's experiences and faith to bring you fresh hope!

—**Dr. Lynne Feller-Marshall,** women's ministry group facilitator of twenty years (Spokane, WA)

This book takes its readers through the situations that shaped Georgia into the strong Christian she is today. Her vulnerability and willingness to share her story are wonderful tributes to God's unfailing love for her and for all of us.

—**Karen Baldwin-Kuntz**

UNFAILING LOVE

FREEDOM FROM ABUSE, SHAME,
AND CONTROL OF A
SCHIZOPHRENIC SPOUSE

UNFAILING LOVE

Georgia Morris

Published by Redemption Press, PO Box 427, Enumclaw, WA 98022, (360) 226-3488.

Redemption Press is honored to present this title in partnership with the author. The views expressed or implied in this work are those of the author. Redemption Press provides our imprint seal representing design excellence, creative content, and high-quality production.

The author has tried to recreate events, locales, and conversations from memories of them. In order to maintain their anonymity and protect their privacy, some names of individuals and places, identifying characteristics, and other details such as physical descriptions, occupations, and places of residence have been changed.

The opinions expressed in this book are those of the author and do not necessarily reflect the opinions of Redemption Press or its editors.

Unless otherwise indicated, all Scripture quotations, are taken from the Holy Bible, New International Version®, NIV®. Copyright © 1973, 1978, 1984, 2011 by Biblica, Inc.™ Used by permission of Zondervan. All rights reserved worldwide. www.zondervan.com. The "NIV" and "New International Version" are trademarks registered in the United States Patent and Trademark Office by Biblica, Inc.™

Scripture quotations marked (AMPC) are taken from the Amplified® Bible (AMPC), copyright © 1954, 1958, 1962, 1964, 1965, 1987 by The Lockman Foundation. Used by permission. lockman.org.

Scripture quotations marked (NASB) are taken from the New American Standard Bible®, Copyright © 1960, 1971, 1977, 1995, 2020 by The Lockman Foundation. Used by permission. All rights reserved. lockman.org.

Italics or bold in Scripture quotations reflect the author's added emphasis.

ISBN 13: 978-1-64645-758-8 (paperback)
978-1-64645-755-7 (ePub)

Library of Congress Catalog Card Number: 2024907914

I dedicate this book to anyone
seeking freedom in their soul. In this life we have trials
that can weigh us down or cause us to want to give up.
May you find hope in casting all or any of your cares
upon the One who sees you and cares. I did—and more
than once, as you'll see when reading this. But my only
complete security has been in the One
I was running from at times.
He continually hugs me with
Unfailing Love.

May you find this love.
May you find hope.
May you begin to be lighter and even smile.
You are valuable and worth His dying
so you can live.

Jesus said in John 10:10,
"The thief comes only to steal, kill, and destroy;
I have come that they may have life,
and have it to the full."

May you have the fullness of
freedom and life on this earth
until we come into His fullness together
in Heaven.

I am forgotten as though I were dead;
I have become like broken pottery. For I hear many whispering,
"Terror on every side!" They conspire against me and plot to
take my life. But I trust in you, LORD; I say, "You are my God."
My times are in your hands; deliver me from the hands
of my enemies, from those who pursue me.
Let your face shine on your servant;
*save me in your **unfailing love.***"

—Psalm 31:12–16

Contents

Acknowledgments

Thank you to the Redemption Press team, who worked diligently, specifically Jennifer Fedler (project manager). Thank you for your encouraging words when I was down or needed to know next steps in this process. You were always quick at responding to my emails in my first attempt to ever write a book. Rachel Bradley (comprehensive editor), I will never forget our first Zoom call! When I met you, you helped pull out of me emotions I didn't even know existed from my depths and helped me express in words what I've lived. We bonded instantly, and now you have become a friend forever. Thank you, Rachel.

I am so grateful for my own children, Jeremy, Joel, Kenny, and Katie. Your love and support have meant everything! I include you Kimberlee and Jenell (daughters-in-law) and Jordan (son-in-law). Your words of encouragement after reading the first manuscript helped me so much!

Thank you, Kenny and Katie, for coaxing me to go deeper. Not only was it therapeutic for me, it brought about more substance for others who will be reading this as well.

And thank you, Katie, for creating the unfailinglovebook.org website! You're so good at it—and quick! Even with your busy schedule, you managed to create links for my songs and designed a place so others can hear our Swoboda music! Love you.

And all of my extended family. (Nick, you helped me record in downtown Seattle—so fun, and I appreciate your time and recording expertise!) I love you all.

Also, close friends in Spokane, where I've lived most of my life and now the Seattle area (Wednesday Warriors, Northwest Christian Writers, Timberlake Church). Special shout out to you, Jill Wolfe in Oregon, for spurring me on when I first began, to let it all out and not hold anything back. It helped so much to begin that digging process. Thank you, Cheri in Colorado, for writing the foreword. What a blessing you are, my forever friend.

And Wes, my amazing husband. You have been so patient and supportive. I always felt you by my side in it all, through prayer, conversation, and love. Thank you for dropping your agenda to snap a picture, create a QR code, or give advice, praying with me and paying for it, Ha! I love you.

Most importantly, I thank my God, who has been there all along with His unfailing love.

Foreword

I have had the honor of calling Georgia my friend and sister in Christ for over forty years. I watched her navigate some incredibly challenging situations; the most difficult were those years in her first marriage dealing with severe mental illness. This book is her story—how through the grace of God and persistent prayer, the Lord brought her through and gave her the courage and support she needed to focus on raising her young sons and walking the path with Christ. Such trials could make someone bitter and angry, but instead Georgia allowed the Lord to use the experience to draw her closer to Him, worship Him, and become an example to those who know her and those who will get a peek into her journey through this book.

I don't know who penned the expression "Do not doubt in the dark what you heard in the light," but this story is a living testament to that instruction. Georgia knowingly chose the difficult path, the path specifically designed *for her* by her Heavenly Father. The Lord has blessed her abundantly for those choices. She is a walking example of "Greater is He who is in you than he who is in the world." (1 John 4:4 NASB).

Georgia's journey will encourage anyone who finds themselves in a difficult situation, wondering how they got there and if there will ever be an end. Staying true to the Path-maker and the path truly brings rewards—not just in the afterlife, but here on earth. This book will provide timely advice and direction to those who may be dealing with mental illness and a great blessing to all who read it!

In a world of Facebook and social media, where the intent is to only put forward the best picture possible, Georgia delivers a refreshing transparency to her life and journey of faith in *Unfailing Love*. The reader will be encouraged by her faith and positive approach to the difficulties of life and will see HIS plans truly are for a "future and a hope" (Jeremiah 29:11 NASB).

I am profoundly grateful for Georgia, her friendship, and all the Lord has done in and through her life!

—Cheri Abraham
BFF and sister in Christ

Preface

When God asked me to write my story, I petitioned Him. "May my eyes be opened to see every little crack of light shining in this dark cave of memories. And may my story bring hope for even one soul who may be in the struggle of life." It took five years to write this book, and I finished it on January 23, 2024. Throughout the process, God has indeed answered my petition, and to Him be the glory for the great things He has done and continues to do.

Through many struggles, I've come to know the only God who can change things, bring growth, and provide true and lasting redemption. I have faith in the power of the blood of Jesus, who is the prime sacrifice sent by God to this earth, giving Himself to make a way for all humanity to have eternal life, and who is King of all kings. He laid down his life at the hands of mankind but rose again! He conquered death and brought true victory to all who choose to believe. I'm convinced He is the way, the truth, and the life (see John 14:6).

I also want to clarify that I have made the choice to capitalize God and references to His name throughout my story. I want to honor Him in this way, and it would be very hypocritical for me, personally, to *not* do this. I have always used capitalization in my journals and any writings referring to God. I want to be authentic to my beliefs. However, when quoting Scripture, I will stay true to the version.

I realize the following memories are just a drop in the ocean of life experiences, but my prayer is that it has an impact for good on the lives and hearts of everyone who is willing to read this. Because so much time has passed in which I've lived free from the ugly days of my past, it was hard to soul search and allow memories I've wanted to forget to resurface. It often felt like warfare on my mind and emotions. But it was worth it for the sake of others who will identify with these memories. Even though we all have different circumstances, we are all human and have feelings. The process of writing my story has been very therapeutic for me, and I pray my story will be equally therapeutic for you, like a tidal wave of hope and faith, washing over and drowning out every tormenting voice and spirit of depression and fear.

Introduction

As deep and many as the painful memories were, there were also joyful times of life and miracles in the seven years I lived with my first husband, Mark. Even though his unstable ways caused a lot of sorrow, the pain drove me to search for help and truth that could set me free. Through prayer, reading the Bible, and the love of people who cared, I began to know the Lord in a very real way as my only strength. He revealed Himself so clearly with His presence. For this, I am forever grateful. He makes all things new and unveils Himself in and throughout the process. During this time, suffering was involved. But in the darkness of the prison of isolation, pockets of brilliance helped me to be able to carry on, one day at a time.

It all started so simply and unexpectedly. I was invited to a dinner at my sister Susie's home in Garden Springs near Spokane, Washington. She and my brother-in-law, Joe, asked if anyone wanted prayer after dinner. Among the five of us, I was the only one that said, "Sure! I can always use prayer!" As a young twenty-year-old, I had many things going on, and I needed direction. Little did I know, my life was about to change drastically with no warning or preparation. That was the night I met Mark.

Before this, there had been many ups and downs in life, like a hopeful heartbeat seen on a heart monitor … until the ups eventually diminished into a flatline. But God was faithful to show His unfailing love, an ever-present help in time of need. The trials were a catalyst for building faith and ultimately led to my freedom, like a chrysalis tightly woven around a butterfly that is eventually set free to fly! I love how Charles Spurgeon describes this process in his devotion for December 30th in *Morning and Evening: The Classic Daily Devotional.* The worm creeps along in the beginning. And then it is sipping at the flower bells with gorgeous wings, playing in the sunbeams, full of happiness and life. I feel like my life has been like this in so many seasons and stages.

CHAPTER ONE

Childhood Treasures

I grew up in a very loving family. My parents were Henry "Hank" and Lois Swoboda. They were both the only children in their families and got married when my dad was finishing his architectural degree at Washington State University (WSU). They had nine of us, one stillborn—my little sister, Debbie Sue. I can't wait to meet her in heaven someday. I am the fifth child. My three oldest sisters, Mary Kay, Susie, and Linda are all one year apart. After them is my brother John, who is two years older than me. I am next in the birth order and then Debbie Sue (it feels good to include her). My three younger siblings are my brothers Jim and Frank and my sister Cathy.

I recently discovered a baby book my mom had put together for me. Most pages were empty, but she made quite an effort with four other children, for sure! Inside was a birth announcement my dad had created like a blueprint.

I found several treasures. I wish my parents were still alive so I could thank them. It just made me so thankful for them. In their busy lives, they worked as a team to love and support us. I have met so many friends who do not have the experience of loving parents. Even as kids, we had friends who wanted to come over to spend time around our family. Even though it could be a chaotic atmosphere, love was preeminent.

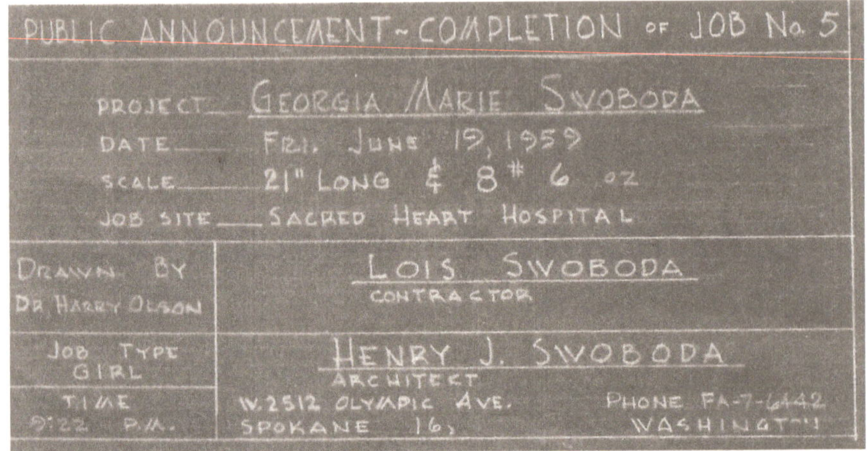

"Completion of Job No. 5," my birth announcement

My parents were both talented musicians and passed that love for music down to all of us. I'm sure they are both still playing music in heaven, even as I write my story.

We had many happy memories in our first home on Olympic Street in Spokane, Washington. My parents were surrounded by neighbors who looked out for one another, including old college friends who lived across the street. Mom told us they took such good care of us during the traumatic time of Debbie Sue's birth. She also said how it was too hard for her to hold her, but my dad did. Debbie Sue had dark curly hair. I have thought that in this day of more advanced medical technology, she may have survived. However, my parents heard she died when my mom was seven months along. I asked her why they didn't take her then. Her reply was, "Well, your dad and I wanted more children, and we were told that if they did a procedure to take her at seven months, it may have made it impossible to have more children." This is another proof of how much love my parents had for all of us and for life itself. My mom carried her for two months, knowing she was dead, while raising five other little ones under the age of seven. I call that sacrificial love. I don't think I could have done that.

When there were just five of us and I was the baby, we would all gather in our cozy living room in our three-bedroom home. My mom would start playing a fast polka on the piano or accordion, and I, as a two-year-old, would spin away, round and round, until I dropped, exhausted with glee! Dad would break out his clarinet or saxophone and join the party. What fun we had!

Christmas and Easter were particularly special. The night before these holidays, Mom would have all four of us girls sitting in the living room with our pj's on.

With my eyelids heavy, I would whimper, "Is it my turn yet?"

Seeing I was falling asleep, she would put me up to the front of the line and carefully twist strands of my golden hair into a tiny swirl, sealing them with two to three crisscrossed bobby pins. It took so long, but Mom was very diligent to make us look pretty. The next day, we would go to Mass with bouncy, tight pin curls, dolled up in fancy clothes. My three older sisters would wear their pink or red matching pony felt skirts, and I would have on a frilly dress. My brother, Johnny, would wear a bow tie and a checkered suit. After Mass, we would come home to have the rest of the celebration. All five of us would sing and dance with delight. When I got tired of dancing, I'd hop on my brown-and-white rocking horse and rock back and forth to the music!

Age two, me and my rocking horse

Both sets of my grandparents would come over, or we would take a Sunday drive to Grandpa and Grandma Swoboda's house, which was only about five miles away on Liberty Street. Ironically, our last name meant "liberty." And they loved to tell the story of how they met in British Columbia, Canada. Grandpa's parents had moved from Czechoslovakia to New York, where Grandpa was born, and then on to Canada when he was two. Grandma's parents had moved to Canada from Yugoslavia. The name *Swoboda* in Czechoslovakia was really spelled Svoboda, but when my grandpa was an adult, he changed the name to Swoboda, because no one seemed to be able to pronounce the *v* in "Svoboda."

After Grandpa's family moved to Nelson, British Colombia, my great-grandfather bought some land, started a farm, and opened a store. Two of my brothers later visited Nelson and discovered that one of the streets there is called Swoboda Street!

Once Grandpa and Grandma married and before my dad was born, they chose July 4th (Liberty Day) to move from Canada to Spokane. They always told us, "The Liberty family moved on Liberty Day to Liberty Street!" Liberty was literally in my blood.

My grandma, Katie Swoboda, was the oldest of thirteen children. She had polio when she was two, and it left her crippled. Her mother wrapped one of her feet so tightly that it never grew well. She had one size-four foot, and the other one was size seven. So she limped around the rest of her life. She was also told she would never have children and should never even think of having children. But she and my grandpa decided to try, and they had my dad! We always say none of our very large family would be here if it wasn't for their decision to have a child. They trusted God, and my dad was born totally healthy.

Even though their house was only five miles away from our home, it seemed much farther with all of us tucked tightly into our station wagon. These days, we wouldn't have fit with car seats. Car seats weren't a thing then; neither were seat belts. But we had seats in the back end that faced

Katie Verzuh, Nelson, BC, 1917 (age eighteen);
My dad and Grandma Swoboda, 1986

each other. Those were usually for the older kids. Grandpa Henry loved making us 7UP floats in small glasses etched with an *S* (for Swoboda). Grandma Katie would bring her little monkey puppet out and make us really believe it was real. It sure seemed like it!

When I was four, I tried so hard to learn how to ride up and down the sidewalk on my very tiny bike without training wheels. Johnny could whip around the corner and ride up the alley with such flare and ease. Why couldn't I? He made it look so easy. After all, he was six! I was determined to be as good as he was on his bike.

On one occasion, he disappeared around the corner to the alley.

"Johnny, where are you? Wait for me!" I sped around the corner, and to my dismay, he skidded his bike down the hill of the graveled alley surface, crashing hard. I screamed. "Mommy! Mommy! Johnny crashed!" After turning my bike around, I made a great effort to stay balanced and pedal quickly while yelling over and over, "Mommy, Johnny crashed!" But I was moving too slowly. I left my bike on the sidewalk and ran around the corner into the house. Mom listened as I sobbed and told her what had just happened, and she ran out to retrieve him. My heart broke in such sadness for him. It turned out he got a concussion but recovered just fine.

Grandma's original monkey with the new monkey
she got when the old was worn out.

Not long after this, we moved to a bigger home on Wellesley that could fit our growing family. My brother Jim, "Jimmy," was born about the time we were getting settled. I was so excited to help with him, and I wasn't the baby anymore.

My dad had his architecture business running strong, and Mom stayed home to raise us. Bringing up eight children was quite the challenge for two people who had grown up with no siblings. Mom went through a time of depression after being worn out from the demands of motherhood. After all, she was an only child. Her life completely changed from performing music to becoming a stay-at-home mother—which she loved, but it was a lot. She relied upon me to care for my younger siblings, especially once my older siblings were gone from home or about to be. Once I got my driver's license, Mom would often say to me, "Take the babies."

I loved my younger siblings but sure grew tired of the responsibility that shouldn't have been mine. (I really do love you *babies*, Frankie and Cathy. You're adorable … it was Mom I had to forgive.) So I determined I'd leave home after graduating and never have kids. As time has passed, and now after raising my own family, I sure treasure the love and sacrifices my parents made for us. I'm *so* very thankful, beyond words, for my children and grandchildren!

At my parents' fiftieth wedding anniversary celebration, Dad shared how, before they got married, my grandma Halfpapp had never taught Mom how to prepare food. When my mom would ask if she could help in the kitchen, Grandma would respond, "Lois, go practice your piano." So on their honeymoon, Mom was thrilled to prepare a meal for Dad on her own. She started by cutting up slices of cucumber and then peeled each slice.

Dad, being the caring man that he was, tapped her on the shoulder and said gently, "Can I show you something, Lois?" Then he took another cucumber and peeled it all and then sliced it. She was so impressed! Oh, the simple things in love that are huge and go so far. My parents loved each other well and demonstrated that to us kids in many ways. ☺

I lived in our home on Wellesley until I graduated high school. My parents lived at least another thirty-five years there before they moved out to something smaller. It was the family home all of us remember, filled with happy, sad, emotional, stressful, whacky, funny, and unforgettable memories.

During these childhood years, I believed in God and even scooted over in my desk at school to make room for Jesus to sit by me. When I walked home for lunch, I'd be so happy and imagined He was holding my hand. I knew He was with me, and He was! His presence was tangible.

Second grade school picture

My favorite spot to go when things got loud was outside on our open concrete deck located off the dining room and above our double-car garage. It had a rail all around it and an orange brick fireplace. Next to that fireplace, I found a little hidden corner that gave a second-story view of the blocks and scenery in front of the house. At times, I even saw the sun setting. It felt so good to see the vastness of the area below while being in a quiet, snuggly place.

Sometimes I would pray. Sometimes I would think up a poem and write it down. Then eventually, I would either burn the words into wooden plaques from the craft store or write them with a permanent marker. Usually, I would select a picture of nature from an old calendar to add life to my poem, for example, a sun shining over grassland filled with sunflowers might accompany "You're like the rays that brighten my days." Then I'd take a white, gluey substance called Mod Podge and brush it over the top to create a shiny, long-lasting surface that would protect my special poem and picture. Once it was dry, I'd sign and date the back. I'd also write personal notes on the back to my mom, my dad, my grandparents, sisters, brothers, friends, or whoever would be privileged to receive one of Georgia's special homemade plaques! They made the perfect birthday or Christmas gift, at least in my mind! I put my heart and soul into making them, and it was a fun way to express myself. Plus, I just knew it was going to really make people happy. And that's all I wanted.

Growing up in a family of ten was always exciting and interesting. In winter, we would pile up snow over the two-leveled flowerbeds in our backyard and pack it down to create a twelve-foot mountain we could try to ski down. My dad had told us he used to ski in his earlier days and wanted us to learn.

One day, he brought home many long wooden skis he bought from a thrift store. He'd have us stand with our hands up and make sure the tip of the skinny wooden ski would be at least that long. Back then, they thought that was the best way, but boy, the shorter ones are so much easier to ski on! Anyway, he showed us what a snowplow maneuver was in the living room, and we would venture out in the backyard on our handmade hill. But when we would try to ski, we'd be down before we could practice the "snowplow move," or we'd fall. Dad decided to help us by showing us how on a real snow hill. There was one at Sacheen Lake, where we'd spend our summer vacations. We started going up in the winter as well on some weekends. They had a small hill, too small for a chairlift but big enough to install a rope tow. This worked to teach us the basics of skiing. My dad was so amazing! He was a real athlete. I learned then that he did more than just go to work. He liked to play! I was so impressed, and he inspired me as a parent to be there for my kids, to play and do things with them. I'm so thankful for the time he spent teaching us. It was truly a sacrifice that paid off!

We also played many a baseball game out in the backyard with our three trees that made perfect bases. I loved climbing one tree especially, but one time our cat got stuck up there, and we had to call the fire department. They came and saved kitty! I didn't climb up there after that.

We had two rooms downstairs for four of us girls. One night, I couldn't sleep and decided I'd crawl across the floor into the other room in the dark where my other two sisters were. When I made it between their two single beds, I rose up with arms raised, shouting, "Boo!"

Everyone screamed! ☺

Give me patience, Lord!

But then came the sound of Dad's foot pounding on the ceiling above us, and that was louder and scarier than my *boo!* It was the signal that quieted everything quickly. Even when we'd try it again, that *thump, thump, thump* came and worked immediately! ☺

As a teenager, I would get up when I couldn't sleep and bake muffins or forage through the cupboards to find something I could try to cook, like tapioca pudding. I had been curious about what it was every time I saw it, but my mom had never made it. So I followed the directions and loved it! Mostly, I liked to invent dishes of different sorts and experiment with food. My dad was my biggest fan at that time. I can still see him in his blue terry cloth robe, coming down the hall at midnight, saying,

"What you cookin' now, Georgie?" And he would sit down quickly and let me serve him and let me know his opinion. Usually, he loved it! Especially muffins and cookies. He even liked the tapioca pudding! He was very encouraging.

Our home on Wellesley was a haven of security and family fun I treasure to this day. We prayed together, watched movies, played games,

She Was Only Child

Mother Feels Child Raising Duty God-Given

Third in a Holy Week series exploring "Religion in the '70s."

By HAZEL BARNES

An only child herself, Mrs. Henry J. Swoboda, mother of eight, feels her task of being a mother and a homemaker is a "God-given one."

Her husband, a Spokane architect, likewise is an only child.

"God put us here with these children, we both feel, to see that they are brought up in the way they should be," said Mrs. Swoboda. Their five girls and three boys range in age from 22 months to 17 years.

And the right bringing up, they realize, includes a firm foundation for life, brought about by faith in God.

"These are pretty troubled times," Mrs. Swoboda pointed out, "and we've found the One to turn to for help is God. Too often, however, He is forgotten."

When troubles or hardships have faced them, both in rearing their children and in carrying on their business, she said, "We've always found it's taken God to bring us through."

"One must remember, though, not to carry the burden on your own shoulders, but to put it in God's hands."

After praying together as a family, particularly when faced with special problems, "God would always bring us through. We must not forget, either, to thank Him for what he's done for us."

Sometimes they've found that God's answer was not exactly the one they were expecting, but it always has proved to be the one that was "right" for their family.

Active members of St. Charles Roman Catholic Church, the Swobodas express their faith, not only by attendance at masses, but in their dealings with each other as well as with others.

A visit to their home at W3104 Wellesley impresses one with the love expressed toward one another and also with the importance the parents place on treating each child as an individual, rather than trying to make them fit the same mold.

Although one youngster had been "grounded" for a minor infraction of family rules, there was no evidence of dislike or hostility toward parents.

No Gap Seen

What about the generation gap? No problem about that in the Swoboda family, for they not only share a faith in God and His importance in their daily lives, but they also share a love of music.

Mrs. Swoboda, the former Lois Halfpapp, and a Marycliff High School graduate, was an entertainer and music instructor prior to her marriage. A gifted accordionist and pianist, she had 30 piano pupils while in high school. Later, while attending Fort Wright College, she had her own studio and taught accordion.

Her husband, a graduate of Gonzaga Prep with his degree in architecture from Washington State University, plays the saxophone and the clarinet.

The husband and wife now have their own five-piece band which plays each weekend in a local lodge hall.

"Music has kept us together as a family, too," said Mrs. Swoboda. "Our children all like music, so we sing and play together a lot and some of the youngsters sing or play instruments for their school programs."

Rearing a family of eight means all have to learn the importance of accepting responsibility, Mrs. Swoboda emphasizes, explaining that each of the older children has his or her own job, which changes on a weekly rotation basis.

Speaking of discipline, she said she and her husband are "tough," making the youngsters toe the line, "but we try to be firm, yet kind, rather than domineering. We think the kids respect discipline, so long as it is given with love."

Vacation time is important, too, in building family "togetherness," the Swobodas have found. With such a large family, they've rented a trailer to go with their station wagon, "but we have never traveled with the two smallest youngsters."

Their favorite recreation spot, summer or winter, is Sacheen Lake and Mrs. Swoboda now has her right leg in a cast, but it's from a fall on an icy path at Sacheen, rather than from skiing.

Mrs. Henry J. Swoboda, her right leg in a cast, is surrounded by her children. In the back, from the left, Georgia, 10, fifth grader at St. Charles' school, and Sue, 15, sophomore; Mary Kay, 17, junior, and Linda, 14, freshman, all at Marycliff High School. In the front, from the left, John, 13, seventh grader at St. Charles'; Cathy (on her mother's lap), 22 months; Frankie, 3, and Jimmy, 8, who is a second grader at St. Charles' school.

Mother of the Year, Spokane

and rehearsed music together as a family. We were even asked to perform at Expo '74, as well as other events. And my mom earned the title "Mother of the Year" in 1970.

I also met my first love at this special home.

CHAPTER TWO

Close to you

One day when I was ten, I turned the record player up loud in my room. Karen Carpenter's romantic voice sang a song about how birds would appear when someone special was nearby ("Close to You," 1970). Standing in front of my grandma's scratched-up vanity dresser with a large mirror that we inherited, I held my fake microphone close to my lips. I knew every word and sang with all my heart to the invisible crowd. After finishing, I ran up the thirteen stairs to the kitchen to get a snack before my concert would continue.

Guitar strumming drifted through the wall between me and the living room, accompanied by the most intriguing soft and raspy voice of an older boy singing. Who was that? *It's definitely not my brother. Hmmmm.* 😊 I crept toward the wall. Most of it was wallpapered with white-and-gold teapots and grandfather clocks, but there were shelves of pictures backed with a plastic sheet made to look like crystalized glass. What did he look like, this new friend of my brother's? He ended the song with impressive harmonics, and then he began singing and playing the song "Fire and Rain" by James Taylor (1968). It was no use; the images through the plastic were beyond fuzzy. I quietly peeked around the corner, and they saw me. 😬 So I had to go in.

There, sitting on the couch with his guitar, was the cutest guy! He had light-brown wavy hair that came to just above his shoulders, nicely shaped. And *he* was nicely shaped! His body was buff and solidly built. He stopped playing and smiled, his sweet, blue eyes crinkling at the edges and his lips revealing nice teeth.

Heat flushed my face, and I barely managed, "What's your name?"

"Jason," he said.

"Oh, I'm Georgia. You sound *so* good." And as quick as a flash, I ran down the stairs. What had just happened? I'd never felt silly and flustered like that. I was smitten, and only as a fifth grader. My heart just melted! The only thing to calm my nerves was to pick up my fake microphone and begin singing again.

My brother had a drum set downstairs in our family room, and I played the piano as he drummed. One day, Jason joined us with his Martin guitar. He was dressed in blue jeans, a white T-shirt, and an oatmeal-colored cashmere sweater. I tried to keep my hands from shaking as I continued playing while we all jammed together. Jason's positive attitude, charming smile, and big heart were irresistible. Everyone in our family loved him, and he quickly became one of my brother's best friends.

His family had just moved to Spokane from California, he attended the same co-ed Catholic elementary school that we went to, and my parents became quick friends with his parents. His dad was a successful real estate agent, and his mom was a stay-at-home mom who was raising three boys, and Jason was the youngest. Over the next few years, we became good friends. They owned a boat and invited our family to go water skiing. When we went on family vacations, I would invite along a girlfriend, and Johnny would bring Jason.

Let's just say ... I began singing songs like "Close to You" with someone in my mind, not just to the invisible crowd.

When I was in seventh grade and he was in ninth (now attending the all-boys Catholic school, Gonzaga Prep), we were vacationing at Hayden Lake, Idaho. We all went on a little walk near the shore. I was trying to pick some little buttercups and wildflowers. Most of the family members with us walked ahead, and he waited for me. I found myself alone with him in the beautiful trees as we walked along the path filled with leaves and flowers. He held out his hand to take mine, and my heart started beating rapidly. I was so very shy, especially in his presence, but his sweet, gentle way invited me in. He seemed to know me, without me having to say anything. His personality was more outgoing and sometimes exuberant, which greatly appealed to me. This innocent love continued with music and friendship, always with family nearby. He had so much going for him, and although he told me all about his friends, I had no idea if his peers knew anything about me. Surely he felt I was like a sister to him, but for me it was more … my heart never beat crazily for my brother!

On one of our walks in the fall, with colorful leaves rustling all around the pathway, he kissed me very gently, ever so slightly. That was enough to seal the deal in my world of fantasy. I was now convinced that someday we would be married! He was my hero and the one for me. I just knew it.

But over the next few years, I kept that expectation safely hidden in my fantasy world. Although Jason wrote me a couple of letters expressing how much he cared for me, even mentioning a couple of times that he loved me, no one knew how emotionally intimate we had become. As long as it was secret, it didn't seem true. I read those letters over and over again, dreaming of the day he would openly declare that we liked each other, instead of keeping it hidden for just the two of us.

When I was sixteen and a sophomore at Marycliff, one of two all-girl Catholic high schools in the area, Jason was a senior at Gonzaga Prep. He was the most popular guy by then, with lead roles in drama and on the football team. When I'd attend his games with the pep club, I'd yell, "Go number fifty-five!" until my throat hurt. Oh, he also was an amazing baseball pitcher and the ASB president. Did I miss anything? Probably.

That year he asked me to go to the prom with him. I was flabbergasted, to say the least! I quickly responded, "Yes!" Wow! It didn't seem real.

My parents did not normally let us kids go on such a date at my age, but because they knew Jason as "part of the family" now, they gave me permission to go. Jason had always been genuine, and I just knew I was safe. He was one I could trust.

With great anticipation, I dressed in my silky black-and-gold fitted sleeveless dress. The skirt reached my ankles, and I wore a matching long-sleeve, empire-waist jacket. My black high-heeled pumps completed the ensemble. I was set!

Jason came with a gorgeous corsage of tiny white roses surrounding a yellow rose. It tied into my colors and had a golden satin ribbon decorating it. I presented him with a matching boutonniere—a yellow carnation surrounded with baby's breath. My mom helped me pin it carefully on his black tux jacket, my parents took photos, and we were off in his navy-blue Nova to meet some friends for dinner before the prom.

Prom was held at the famous Spokane Davenport Hotel. We danced to an amazing live band and then there was the big announcement. We (Jason and I) had been nominated as royalty. The four couples chosen came up to the stage area, and lo and behold! Jason and Georgia were now the prom king and queen. Phew! I had so many friends coming up and congratulating me. Some of the senior girls (Jason's age) didn't say much, but their snickers said tons. So many of the seniors would have loved to be in my shoes, but they weren't—it was little ole me! And a sophomore at that. Life couldn't have been better, or so I thought.

After an amazing evening, we left elated. He drove me home, and on the way he said, "Let's go to my house first before I take you home. My parents went to an event and won't be home for a while."

I agreed, and we happily went to his house. No one was there, and we went downstairs to the basement. He had a pool table there adjacent to his room, and we played for a short bit, talking about how the night went. Then we went into his room and sat on the edge of his bed.

"Wasn't that an amazing night, Georgia? You look so beautiful, and I loved dancing with you."

"Oh yes, Jason, I'll never forget it. And we won the vote for king and queen! Thank you so much for asking me."

After some more talking, he kissed me, and we kissed some more. Pretty soon we were even more physical, and one thing led to another. Things continued until … well, we didn't stop. That was my first time to go all the way (as we put it then), to my much-regretted disappointment.

With only a sheet covering us, Jason mumbled, "Do you hear something?"

"I don't think so."

Suddenly, headlights shined through the window. "Oh no! Now what do we do, Jason?"

His parents' car rumbled as it pulled up into the driveway and then went silent. Scrambling, we tried to tidy up but realized there was not going to be enough time. We did not want to encounter them. I quickly threw on my prom dress and grabbed my purse and shoes.

"You'll have to go out the window here," he said, and he lifted me up through the basement window.

Wait. We needed a reason for him to leave the house. I handed him my purse. "Here. Tell them I forgot it, and you need to take it to me."

With shoes in hand, I waited behind a bush on the side of the house. After the garage door was completely shut, I dashed to the passenger side of the car and got in ever so quietly. (It was rare to lock car doors at that time.) About ten minutes later, Jason came out in a sweatshirt and lounging pants. He'd fixed his bushy hair a bit, so it wasn't quite as disheveled as when I'd left him. He climbed into the driver's seat.

"How'd it go?" Had his act been convincing enough to deflect any suspicion?

"It went great. They had no problem with my running this back to you, and they are super excited for our winning king and queen."

We headed home. Initially, it was kind of fun to think we'd gotten away with something. This was a secret adventure we shared. But as we closed the distance to home, my feelings became mixed in many ways. I was mostly disappointed, conflicted, and traumatized by what had just occurred. But it would all work out, right? He would be my husband someday, and everything would be okay. Guilt and sadness overwhelmed my efforts to justify myself. Oh, why did this perfect night have to end up like this? This was *not* what I was expecting. To drown out the turmoil, I clung to the rest of the night that had held such great and exciting memories.

This is just the beginning, I rationalized over and over to myself. We were a real couple now that Jason had taken me to the prom, and everyone had validated us by voting us royalty. Plus, it was perfect timing before he graduated and moved to Pullman for college. I was *his* now. And he was *mine*!

Since we went to different high schools, we didn't see each other again right away. One week later, there was a mixer, a dance held at the gym of Gonzaga Prep that included my high school and the other all-girls Catholic high school in the city, Holy Names. I couldn't attend because I was singing with my parents' band. This mixer was one of the last ones the seniors would be at before they graduated.

When I went to school that following Monday, several friends came up to me. "Georgia, did you hear? Jason was dancing with Belinda from Holy Names; you know, that popular one? And we saw them leave together!"

The word spread like wildfire! When I asked my brother who she was, he informed me that she was the most gorgeous senior girl at that school, the most talked about among the guys. Wow … my heart sank. All my hopes and dreams drained away. I was like a popped balloon, swirling every which way with hurt, anger, confusion, and betrayal until the air completely left, dropping me into a shriveled mess on the ground.

CHAPTER THREE

Choices and Regrets

Guilt and shame did their work on my mind and emotions. My way of coping was to get busy—push down those feelings and finish out my sophomore year at Marycliff. That next year, Gonzaga Prep became co-ed, and I jumped at that opportunity to attend. Being at an all-girls school had become tiresome, and additionally, my dad had gone to high school at Gonzaga Prep. Now I could say I went two years to my mom's high school and two to my dad's! That felt pretty cool, and that doesn't always happen. I joined choir, drama, and the golf team, in addition to all the rest of the required subjects.

Outside of school, I ushered at Spokane Opera House with girlfriends, where I met Captain and Tennille! We worked shows such as Liberace and Up with People. I almost got run over once, because no one told me the performers would run down the aisles to get up on the stage, singing with great enthusiasm! I nearly got plastered! The symphonies were especially enjoyable, since the timpani player was the drummer for our family's band. I even worked Elvis's last tour. Elvis had his show at the Spokane Coliseum, and I stood with my little gold suit and was supposed to keep all the women from charging up to the stage. I had no idea what would happen.... I knew who Elvis was, but I really didn't think people would scream and yell like they did in the '50s—until I almost got trampled! I had to call for a policeman to come over and help me. Along with this job, I sang some weekends with my parents' band, which I loved.

Through all this time, I didn't really date or have any boy crushes because I still felt crushed. 😞 Despite my best efforts, I never forgot about Jason. Even though the hurt was there, I still missed him. I missed our friendship.

In the summer, I got a job at a place called the Burger Palace, which is no longer there. It was at the Shadle mall, which was only about a mile up the street from our home.

My boss and his wife were interesting. She was very sweet, but he never smiled and was so serious. I decided to prove that I was a hard worker, so I took orders with enthusiasm, scrubbed dishes, wiped the counters, made milkshakes, and cleaned the grill—all with a positive attitude and a smile whenever appropriate. My boss was a very tall man with a bald head, about sixty, and he was always watching me from the back where he cooked hamburgers. I'd see one eye on me and the other on his cooking, if that's possible. Later, after my second summer there, I had to stop working. They both sat me down and told me that anytime I needed anything, they were there!

I was surprised, to say the least, especially by him. "I thought you didn't really like me."

"Why?" he asked.

"Well, because I never saw you smile … you always looked so serious."

"Well, Georgia, that's because I saw something in you. You have great potential! You could run this place. Judy and I were actually thinking maybe we could turn this over to you someday. We're sad to see you go."

That was a compliment I never saw coming, and it really goes to show that we don't always know what's behind a serious face.

At our senior prom, all the memories of two years earlier came flooding back. Lots of my girlfriends didn't have dates, so instead of going with any of the guys from our class, we decided to go together. They say things come in cycles; well, here it came again for me. At the prom, I ended up with a guy I never should have been with—I still wasn't healed from everything with Jason. After all, if Jason could be wild, so could I! The sad part about all that is, in the end, I was just playing revenge on Jason … revenge that only hurt me and this guy. Many years later, I did see him and took the opportunity to ask for his forgiveness. That may have seemed odd to him then from so many years before, but nevertheless, I needed to ask.

That year, I got the lead role in *South Pacific*, Nellie Forbush. I was coached by my drama coach and a Broadway actress who had played Nellie. We did not have clip-on microphones, so I had to learn to project my soft voice to the corners of the gym, where each one of them would stand. And there were so many lines to memorize! But I learned quickly, and it was one of the best memories I have of my high school years. They even made a real shower on the stage for my song, "I'm Gonna Wash That Man Right Outa My Hair." We performed two weekends of shows, and it was a hit! I was finally getting noticed, but more than that … I had accomplished something that used all the talent I could muster to entertain people! And I became popular, but that faded quickly because we went in all directions when we graduated.

That summer, I turned eighteen and was excited to be starting classes at the community college soon. But my life suddenly took an unexpected dive. There was a pool in our neighborhood owned by three of the neighboring families. I was invited to a pool party there. We all snacked on chips around the pool and had fun swimming and playing water volleyball.

As the sun was setting, one of the guys, Jake, said to the group of us, "Hey everybody, we have pizza at my house if you all want to come."

Jake and his family were one of the owners of the pool and fairly new to the neighborhood. I had never been in his house before.

Up to that point, we had only eaten chips, so we were hungry. As I was changing out of my swimsuit with the other girls, only two of my girlfriends said they were staying. I felt okay with staying for a bit as well. What was his house like, I wondered? I didn't live too far away, so I could probably get a ride from somebody.

After we went in, more people started showing up that weren't at the pool party. They were all older than me and my girlfriends.

"The pizzas are in the oven, so let's get this party started!" Jake shouted, tossing his shoulder-length dishwater-blond hair. He proceeded to get out cans of beer, saying with glee, "I'm so glad my parents are gone for the weekend!"

His dad had recently been stationed in Laos and had just returned to the States. Jake was proud of showing us some marijuana that he believed came from Laos. I was not a pot smoker and had only tried it one time.

Where was this headed? I turned to one of my friends. "Theresa, should we leave?"

"No, I'm staying," she replied.

The pressure weighed heavy. If I didn't smoke it, I would be the only one not smoking it. It was the moment of truth, and I had to make a decision. I could have said no. I could have left the whole scene. But I didn't have the courage. As the night progressed, we ended up in a dark basement room with paneled walls, smoke filling the air. People were drinking, and it was getting louder and louder. After I tried the pot, everything became a blur—an absolute nightmare of a blur! It was either a very potent drug, or someone may have slipped something into my drink. The world became hazy, almost slow motion.

I can't remember any details, but by the time things cleared, I was in a state of shock. My stomach churned with nausea, and my head pounded. It wasn't until a bit later that I realized I had had sex with Jake against my will, not wanting to at all … but I had no strength or care to fight against it. I was so weak and was definitely not in my right mind. I would call this rape now, but at that time, no one ever called it what it was. It seemed to be the accepted thing to do in the '70s. It was hard to even fathom what had happened. Jake took me home afterward, and I just wanted to forget everything. I wanted to hide under my covers forever! I didn't even like him! He was gross. It was an absolute nightmare. Shame overwhelmed me, and I was disgusted with myself … but I also felt like I couldn't tell anyone, because it was *my* mistake. I totally blamed myself. For a time, I even tried to completely deny it happened at all, even blocking the memory for many years. It was a dark secret I never wanted to face or have revealed. Years later, after experiencing emotional healing, I understood that shame and hiding become a prison in our souls. The Lord shines His light of love to expose our darkest sins for our *freedom*, and exposing those dark places to His marvelous light actually breaks the power shame has over us. In facing the truth, we can be set free. At that time, I was not even close to being aware of this, but it is the very situation that caused me to plead with God for His mercy and forgiveness.

Since that time, He has shown me His unfailing and perfect love. Isaiah 54:10 says, "'Though the mountains be shaken and the hills be removed, yet my *unfailing love* for you will not be shaken nor my covenant of peace be removed,' says the LORD, who has compassion on you." He wants our best, and for that reason, He lets us know the truth even if we try to run. I was doing everything to try to make it all go away, and *I was running*! Little did I know, I would be running from my fears into *His* arms of love. His *unfailing* and *unconditional* arms of love. His arms of undeserved forgiveness.

A few weeks later, my great-aunt Helen (my grandma's youngest sister) and Uncle Stan who lived in Sacramento, California, gifted me with a trip for my graduation to visit them for two weeks there. This was an extremely generous gift! It was also unusual for me to go anywhere by myself, especially to fly on an airplane and be in sunny California for two weeks! I thought the timing was perfect for an escape from this horrible pit I found myself in. I accepted with joy!

The trip wouldn't happen for a couple of months, and in the meantime, Jake and I saw a little of each other. It seemed easier to pretend nothing had happened if things were "normal" between us. During those two months, I didn't have a period, which was very odd for me.

Before I left for California, my sister Susie and I were asked to sing for a Christian concert with two brothers from a different family. I told her I wasn't really sure about it. There was a battle going on in my soul, as I still felt unworthy to even be around a Christian event, let alone help lead worship. She gave me a cassette tape of Christian songs to listen to and try to learn while I was on my trip.

When I boarded the airplane to Sacramento, I became extremely frightened that I might be pregnant! On the airplane, I begged God for His mercy like never before. I was so mad at myself…. I was repulsed by Jake and knew there was no way I could ever see or be with him again. Plus, I had just turned eighteen and just graduated high school! He was twenty-one. I begged God, pleading with everything in me to have mercy on me and on this baby inside me and to please take it back to heaven. I was so sorry for what I had allowed and so afraid! Not long after I prayed this on the airplane, I had to get off for one layover in Portland. During this layover, I visited the restroom and discovered I had started bleeding so hard, like never before. God had heard my cry! I hadn't even been in the habit of praying much at all during this time of my life. Could it really be that He heard my prayer? Yes, it was true, and I was miscarrying this little life inside of me. God was really with me, and I felt His presence—strong, comforting, and mind-boggling at the same time!

The fear of the Lord overtook me. I mean *fear* as reverence and awe that God is and was so real! He heard my prayer ... little me! The God of the universe heard my prayer! I always believed He was a good God, but this? For me? And for this baby? Could He be such a personal and merciful Father that had my best interests at heart and the best interests of this little life that was forming inside of me? It gripped me like no other time, and this experience spurred me on to make many life changes ahead.

CHAPTER FOUR

Sacramento Break Away

I loved soaking up the sun in Auntie Helen's backyard in sunny California those two weeks. As relieving as it was, the miscarriage left me feeling traumatized again, but I could not fathom sharing this experience with anyone, especially my great-aunt and uncle. I just couldn't believe what I had done and what had just been undone. It was an extremely emotional time for sure.

Music had always been therapy for me and brought a lot of peace and joy. Therefore, I listened to songs on my cassette recorder and radio to help drown out the voices of guilt and disgust playing in my mind as I basked in the sun, alone in the backyard in sunny Sacramento. In contrast to the feelings of despair, it was so enjoyable and relaxing to just be there by myself. Susie's insistence that I listen to the Christian songs we were asked to sing kept coming back to mind. So I vacillated between listening to secular music and spiritual music.

I know God was working on my heart and using this opportunity to draw me closer to Him, but there was a real fight inside of me. I'd completely blown it! It was one thing, and super difficult, to forgive Jake. But how could I ever forgive *myself*? It seemed impossible.

After my two-week stay with my relatives, my sister Susie and my younger brother Jim drove down from Spokane to Sacramento to pick me up and bring me back home. Susie was twenty-three and had her own car. Jimmy was almost sixteen years old and so excited to accompany her on this fun adventure and help her drive. He had his permit and would get his license about a month after getting back home.

On the road trip home along the Pacific Ocean, we stayed at the Big Lagoon County Park. Early the next morning, I went out alone on the beach and gazed at the powerful waves and beautiful sunrise. Peace flooded my soul and filled me with awe. No one else was around, and I felt so very small. I realized that almighty God was wanting me to not just see and experience His beauty but also see and experience how much He loved me. My past decisions did nothing to change that love, His *unfailing love*. I drew in a breath of His bigness and thanked Him for His awesome creation all around me. His presence became tangible as I stood there alone. Miles of beach stretched on each side of me, and ocean waves rolled with thunderous crashes in front of me. He wanted me to understand that I was His creation, and just like I was loving every minute of these precious moments, He was delighting in what He saw ... me!

With arms outstretched wide, I said to Him, "You see me, don't You?"

A quiet hush fell all about me. He was incomprehensibly big, and I was like one of the tiny grains of sand at my feet. "How can you love me? I've been such a mess, such a hypocrite. I've lived a lie, presenting an image to my parents and friends that I'm so good. And yet, *You* know me; *You* see me as I really am! You've been with me all along and seen everything. And yet, You still love me?"

I could feel His mighty presence ... knowing that He saw me standing there. The comfort and awesomeness of God Almighty that I felt right then and there is beyond description. I just knew without any doubt that He forgave me and loved me beyond human love! But could I forgive myself?

It was breathtaking, and His complete peace wrapped around my feeble self. The Father was drawing me, and I understood more than ever Jesus's words in John 6:44 (NASB), "No one can come to Me unless the Father who sent Me draws him; and I will raise him up on the last day." He was raising me up that moment from my dead life. I could now authentically grow into a new life, one that He was gently loving me into.

I decided to sing the concert with Susie and the two brothers. ☺

When I got back to Spokane, I told Jake about the miscarriage, even though our relationship was purely superficial, and I broke off all ties with him. Although staying at that party was a huge mistake that I deeply regretted, it created the very situation of fear, weakness, and failure within myself that caused me to desperately call out to God for help. I couldn't help myself or perform to make myself feel better or cover up my sin. Only God's divine intervention could set me free, and He was there for me.

Not long after returning to Spokane from the California trip, I moved out from my parents' home and into a small house about a mile away from them with my sister Linda and her four-year-old daughter Heather, my precious little niece. I bought my first car, a tan Toyota Corona, after saving money from my usher job at the Spokane Opera House, Burger Palace, a dry-cleaning business, and singing engagements with the Swoboda Family Band: wedding receptions, Spokane Club, Elks Club, Moose Club, Catholic parish dances, Elkins Resort on Priest Lake, and even recording a CD together. (Here is a link to that for you to enjoy! https://soundcloud.com/swoboda-family-band)

I also started my first year at Spokane Falls Community College (SFCC). Things seemed to be going so well that fall of 1977. But what a summer it had been … one to forget and one to always remember.

Even though I had had the experience on the ocean, I still was not fully walking on the right path, and I knew it. I ended some bad relationships (some not shared in this book), but I still felt very vulnerable and compromised in ways I did not want to be. My only support system was my sister Susie who had recently experienced God in a very real way. She had begun attending a church that wasn't Catholic called Christian Life Center. I was still attending the Catholic church but started going to her church as well. The first time I attended, I was nervous, but I'll never forget the way everyone burst out in song, all singing with everything they had to the Lord! It was what I used to long for, even as a little girl! I loved the hymns and singing in the church I grew up in, but this was another level. People seemed excited and genuine about the worship, and there was such life! It really impacted me in a new way that I loved. I was thankful my sister Susie had the courage to go experience something new outside the Catholic church. She took a lot of flak for it. She was the first person I knew in many generations of our family who did something like this.

One afternoon as I pulled up to the house I lived in with Linda, I noticed a party going on in our backyard. A weird hesitation came over me, and I didn't want to go into the house. I didn't know exactly why, so I stayed in my car and prayed. My fear only grew, and I decided I should go in and call my sister Susie. In 1977 we did not have cell phones, so I ran into the kitchen, which had no one in it, and called her. She suggested we meet in a park. I agreed and ran back to my car. When I looked out in the backyard, I had such a bad vibe. There was a group of friends over for a barbecue. Several people that I knew were there, but their faces looked very strange, sort of demonic, or like mean creatures you might see in a sci-fi movie. I'm not referring to my sister Linda but just a mixed group of people we were familiar with. It only lasted for seconds, like a blur. All I knew was that it gave me an eerie feeling and I had to get away. I blinked my eyes a few times to make sure I was seeing correctly. I thought I was going crazy! Nothing changed. I had never seen anything like this before. A few looked normal, but some had that weird look. It scared me enough that I left for the park as quickly as I could.

CHAPTER FIVE

The Greater One

As I walked through the park to meet Susie, people all around were enjoying the sunny day. I reached her, and we sat down on the grass. She asked if she could pray with me and reached for my hands. That was very awkward because my first thought was, *They're going to think we're lesbians*. But as soon as I held her hands, I had peace and closed my eyes.

What took place after that was like a motion picture. I saw a little black dot slowly falling away with two big, gray walls closing in on it. I knew the dot represented me, and I could not stop the cement-looking gray walls from closing in…. I could actually feel the pressure of these walls as they drew closer. Even though I tried to open my eyes, I couldn't! It was very strange. I told Susie what was happening.

She said, "Georgie, just give your hundred percent to Jesus; you need to give your all to Jesus," and she repeated that a few times.

The walls kept pressing in, about to smash the black dot. I felt as if I would physically die if they continued. My heart escalated with rapid beats, and I struggled to breathe. In agony, I said, "I can't promise that. I know I will fail, and I don't want to be a hypocrite!"

"Just call out to Jesus, and He will help you."

In my desperation, every part of my being cried out from deep within my soul, "Jesus!" I said nothing more than that one precious word. Immediately, my eyes opened without even trying, and I saw colors like I had never seen before! Everything was so beautiful, and the awkward fear of what others in the park might think completely subsided and changed to an immense feeling of peace.

Soon after this experience, Susie left Spokane to travel across the country to become involved with a children's ministry. I needed spiritual support and godly friendships, so I began singing with a worship team called Lord of Love Community that consisted of two married couples. We led worship at the Friday night chapels at Gonzaga University. I thought joining this worship team would be ideal, since music was my passion—specifically, singing to the Lord. ☺ There were sometimes up to four hundred people who attended the Friday night prayer meetings.

At some point I said, "You know, I keep thinking drums would sound great with these guitars and piano. I think that would be a great addition." As I mentioned in an earlier chapter, I had grown up playing piano down in our basement with my brother John accompanying me on drums. He was a fantastic drummer (and still is).

A week later, someone who wasn't on the worship team but heard us talking about wanting to add drums handed me a check for four hundred dollars and commented to me, "Go buy a drum set!"

I responded, "Awesome! Now who's going to be the drummer?"

All five people instantly looked at me and said, "Well, we guess you are!"

I did have a little experience in playing, thanks to my brother who taught me, but this was really the first time for me to play with a group. I learned as I went, singing as I played along. I loved every minute, even hauling them up three floors in a small elevator every Friday night. They fit perfectly in my little Toyota. And the drum set and I could just fit into the elevator. And guess what? It was a set with Zildjian cymbals (considered the best at the time) for four hundred dollars!

We also played for retreats and youth rallies around Washington and Idaho. The new charismatic movement was taking place within the Catholic church, and it was so exciting and fresh after what we were used to in just attending Mass on Sundays. I began to connect with others and formed healthy relationships. I also joined my dad, playing piano and singing while he played upright bass along with a couple of others at our St. Charles Parish church, the one I grew up in and attended eight years of school at. We were the "folk Mass" on Saturday nights, and I loved that too!

Jason would come home from WSU during the summers and reach out to me. Early on, we met, and I told him that I could not have the type of relationship we had before, when I was sixteen. I shared with him about my experience with the Lord and that I really wanted to stay pure from now on before marriage. He honored that but said it was difficult to hear because he really wanted me to move in with him at WSU. He said he didn't have a girlfriend. I told him I couldn't live with him. It wasn't right. The Bible says it's sin … fornication, as we had both learned growing up in the Catholic church.

We were very good friends, and I still adored him, but I couldn't compromise what I had promised the Lord. It's strange to think about now, but at the time, if he would have proposed, I would have said yes. I still had such a heart of love for him. I'm so glad he didn't ask me because now I have been married almost thirty-four years to my true love, Wes, the man God had for me. I see that clearly now in so many ways. He truly has blessed me with the desire of my heart … but at that time, I couldn't see past this relationship that meant so much.

I lived with my sister Linda and my niece Heather for one year. After that year, I moved out to my first apartment, which wasn't far from where I grew up. I loved this one-bedroom apartment! My parents had given me the piano I grew up with, and my dad helped move it in. I played worship songs, wrote new songs, read my Bible, really for the first time on my own. I had grown up hearing sermons from the priests at Mass, which would include Scriptures, and learned some Bible in religion classes. Something new was happening, though, to where I sometimes couldn't stop reading, and the Holy Spirit was making it come alive! I just loved my time there, and I started my second year of college as well at SFCC. Playing the piano, singing, and making up songs of praise to God became a huge passion of mine. Living by myself provided a place free from distractions. God was talking directly to me, and I was learning more and more about how to listen and how alive He really is—not just a God who lived in the past. Not a God way up in heaven looking down. Not an unapproachable God. Not a God who expected duties and works performed to earn acceptance. He became personal and my very best friend. I could talk to Him about anything, and He listened! His presence was all around me like a warm blanket. I felt very comforted, cleansed, and forgiven; although strong battles for my soul, wanting me to go a different direction, continued.

During the summer before my second year of college, Jason asked me for a date. I can honestly say I was so excited, and it was like we had everything there together … except the most important element. We couldn't share a mutual deep love for God. As much as I tried, there just was not a common bond spiritually. Even though he had been raised Catholic and said he believed in God, there was just something different between us when it came to faith. He didn't have the same desire to *live* for God, with Jesus as the center of his life.

I was happily settled in my new apartment. He came there to pick me up for our date. We had dinner and went to a movie, and he asked me several times to come to Pullman and live with him. He said he loved me. There was no way I was at peace about moving in with him. After seeing the movie, he came back to my apartment. We talked for a while, and he started to kiss me. I was hesitant, because I really did not want to violate my conviction to be sexually pure before the Lord, as I had resolved to be at that time in my life. I reminded him of my convictions, but he continued kissing me and said that's all that would happen. But in moments, he had me down on the floor, and I knew things were not stopping. I had just been taught the Scripture, "Greater is He who is in you than he who is in the world" (1 John 4:4 NASB), and I knew that "he who is in the world" referred to temptation and the devil and how the devil wanted to destroy my faith and commitment to God. The devil was using my vulnerability to tempt me with something I really wanted. Resisting him was so hard but so right. I looked into Jason's blue eyes and began praying inside. He stopped kissing me and looked at me a bit strangely. In my mind, I quoted that Scripture, and he got up, got his coat, and said peacefully, but a bit startled and with a confused expression, "I have to go now, Georgia."

I never saw or heard from him again until over twenty years later at his mom's funeral. He had become vice president of a nuclear company—very successful, which is what he always wanted. He had a wife and four kids, three girls and one boy. I had already happily married Wes, and we had three boys and one girl (Jeremy, Joel, Kenny, and Katie). After the funeral, I went to his parents' home with my dad and brother for a dinner that followed. That was awkward at first because I hadn't been inside much, if at all, since that prom night. I met his family, and as I was leaving, he asked if he could walk me out.

As we got to the outside porch, he said very genuinely, "You know, Georgia, I have always loved you."

It was a very precious moment, and it meant a lot to me. I felt like I wasn't just being used by him all that time and that there really was a genuine love between us back in those days. We hugged and I went on my way. I felt like a giant tear in my heart from long ago was mended.

After I achieved an associate of arts degree from SFCC, I started going to Eastern Washington University (EWU) to get my bachelor of arts degree. My grandma died, and two girlfriends and I moved into her home in the Gonzaga area. This was my mom's home as a young girl, and my parents were happy to let us rent it. We revamped the house inside, tearing all the wallpaper down in the living room, which had consisted of big green leaves and red roses. We painted the whole inside of the house, upstairs and down. Upstairs was a little area that I used to play in while staying with Grandma. We converted it to a prayer room with lots of pillows, candles, and a small table we put under the window with flowers and a Bible. It became our little chapel. ☺

I was enjoying college, working part time for my dad as the secretary of his architecture business and continuing to serve at Gonzaga on Friday nights, singing and playing drums. The group would practice a few times a month in the GU district (the area in proximity to Gonzaga University) at the home of one of the couples on the team. We would drive around Washington state to small towns, providing worship music for youth groups and retreats.

I was thrilled and so happy! Until …

One day as I typed away for Dad, a man I had never seen before came in the office and introduced himself. He said he was just moving in down the hall with his dental-lab business. He was looking for someone like me who they could train with pay as a dental-lab technician.

I thought that would be pretty cool! Several days went by, and I decided to take the job.

CHAPTER SIX

Feeling Trapped

Except for sitting all the time, learning how to make gold crowns and dentures was fascinating. I polished dentures mostly on a machine, but making the crowns was my favorite! I sat at a Bunsen burner in my own area and melted wax, bead by bead, to form what looked like a mountain. Then I made grooves in the wax with different size tools, taking moments to squash down the impression mold of the person's mouth to fit and carve it just right before placing it under the white-hot fire that spun around, melting the wax, and then throwing the melted gold into the area the wax had been to form the gold crown. I had to wear special welding goggles. I loved it all! I even got to create my own gold crown, which I still have in my mouth now. I carved it and put my initials in, G. S. for my maiden name—Georgia Swoboda. Yep! It's now over forty years old and still standing with no problems. ☺ It may be time to take it out, and I'm pretty sure my seven grandchildren will fight over it, ha ha!

My excitement for the job, not the work but the atmosphere, quickly changed. The basement level of the building had been occupied only by Dad's architecture business and one other small realty company for the past thirty-five-plus years. One day, I went into the only bathroom on the basement level. To my surprise and dismay, there were *Playboy* magazines on the back of the toilet! I *knew* it wasn't my dad who put them there. He was a very righteous man, living by moral standards. The Realtor was also a very trustworthy person. We knew him and his family well. The only other business using that bathroom was the dental lab, which consisted of my boss and me, and sometimes the owners who would pop in, a married couple. I told Dad what I had discovered. He handled it and talked to my boss, who admitted to it. Dad told him to take them out. He did. This incident, right or wrong, left a desire in me to share about my newly found spiritual life and conversion with this man. After all, the spiritual input I was getting was so good, and I desired with all my heart to share it with others. So I began to talk to my boss, Rob, about my faith.

He was kind of a gruff person but seemed to also have a giant heart, if that makes sense. When I shared my experiences, he listened intently and seemed genuinely interested, and I appreciated that. He smoked cigarettes a lot, drank after hours, and had quite a foul mouth on him—I could tell he had had a rough past. But overall, he seemed to be really nice and caring.

I can't remember the details now, but I was going through some rough things in my life at the time, and he asked me to share them. He was the most caring listener, and I felt I could share anything with him. The more we talked, the more it seemed like he wanted to clean up his act and draw closer to God. This encouraged me. My parents had Rob, his wife, and their two teenagers over to their house a few times. And he ended up getting baptized in the Catholic church.

Sometimes he would give me these big bear hugs that were very comforting, especially after I'd share a rough experience. I began trusting him and seeing good changes happening in him. He seemed happier. It was exciting because that's what my prayer and my heart were for him. My parents and I were having a good influence on him.

Then it all changed.

After work on a Friday, he asked if I could stay a bit and talk in the lobby. Everyone had left the building. I told him I needed to go. He wouldn't take no for an answer and started talking. It was getting dark, maybe around six o'clock. When I said again that I really had to go, he took me down on the floor and began kissing me. He was very strong, and when I resisted and tried to push him off, he got angry and refused to stop. He reeked of beer!

I managed to distract him and got up and ran out the front door and up the concrete stairs in front of the office. But he ran after me, and before I reached the top, he pulled me down the stairs, pushed me back into the office, and locked the inside door with the master key, so I could not unlock it from the inside and get out. It was so scary! His face was very red and angry. He pushed me back down on the floor, then at one point told me he had to go to the bathroom.

He said, "You better stay there! You can't get out anyway!"

After he left, I quickly got up and ran to the nearest office phone (still not having cell phones around). I fiercely jabbed the buttons of my dad's number at home. He was the only other person who had a master key to that door.

In a frantic whisper, I said, "Dad, come to the office. Rob locked me in here with him. Hurry!"

Then I rushed back to the lobby just in time before Rob came back. I immediately engaged him in conversation, stalling him until Dad could get there. Finally, Dad and one of my brothers arrived and unlocked the door. My dad was furious when he came in, and he verbally blasted Rob.

As I write this out, forty years later, I vaguely remember other traumatic instances with Rob. I am not sure whether they were before this incident or after. Regardless of what order, he raped me several times during the time I worked for him. I felt so trapped. I told myself that I was wrong and that there was no way I had the courage to come out and tell anyone … after all, I was an adult now. How embarrassed I would be to face the truth, and I felt like it would be easier to just not say anything. But things escalated. If only I would have had the courage to say something to someone, anyone I trusted, and even to press charges. Fear took hold of me, and once again, shame and disgust tormented me. I convinced myself that it was *my* fault. That lie gripped me into numbness. I just wanted to get out of this mess and away from him. My mind filled with hopelessness. *Why was this happening to me?* I continued working for him, which was a huge mistake, but he seemed to be different, even though he wasn't.

I urge you, no matter what age you are, even as an adult, young or old, please don't let dark secrets keep you bound. All of us are vulnerable if we keep things hidden that should be exposed. As I have lived now as a parent of four, I also urge you parents to please tell your kids, no matter how young or old they are, that when someone does something to them and hurts them, violates them in any way and they feel wronged, especially when that someone tells them *not* to tell anyone, that's when they *should!* If someone threatens in any way, that's when you tell someone you trust. I'm convinced that cycles of sin can be broken if they come out into the light. Plus, we can live freely instead of continually tormented.

Finally, one day, I thought, *I've got to come really clean and get rid of this man.* I was so desperate and decided to go to his wife and tell her what was happening. I had to confess my part in this situation. So I went to the hair salon she worked at, and she took some time to listen.

After I told her the truth and asked her forgiveness, she said a very strange thing to me. Her voice was full of disappointment. "Oh, I was really hoping *you* were going to be the reason I could finally be free of him. Did you know Rob has a past of being in prison? I've always wanted to leave him. I was really hoping you'd be the way for me to be free from him."

Her response was so very creepy. I thought she'd hate me and be really upset! Very sad for her. And his having been in prison was news to me. It made me all the more determined to get out of this dangerous and sick situation.

I quit my job. It was a nightmare. When I told him, he was so angry that he threw a plant that was in a glass pot at me. I dodged it, barely. He had my address from employment and knew where I lived with my two friends. He never came in, but for some weeks after I quit, he would drive by the house, and a couple of times we saw him outside the window of my room. He was stalking me. On a couple of occasions, a neighbor and I had to call the police. It was such a fearful time. I wish now that I had pressed charges, but I was just relieved to have him out of my life.

Music was such a therapy for all this. I was so glad to be part of the Lord of Love Community. We continued traveling around Washington and Idaho to lead retreats and services. On one occasion, we played for Cataldo Mission in Idaho and about two hundred people came. It was two days of amazing worship and fellowship—a healing balm to my broken soul. We had a van for most of the equipment and my Toyota that carried my drums, but our hope was to purchase a milk truck or something big enough to fit everything.

CHAPTER SEVEN

My Little Flower

After leaving the dental lab, I attended a silent retreat at Immaculate Heart Retreat Center on Spokane's South Hill. It was a very special and safe place to me, as I had gone many times on retreats with my mom or groups, but this time I went alone. While I was there, we had a chapel time that was about the need to give ourselves wholly to God. The priest encouraged us to go back to our rooms and take the next two hours to pray and think about what we wanted to surrender to the Lord. Then we were to bring something symbolic of that to place on the altar when we returned.

So I decided to sit outside on the sunny deck off of my room, looking out over the vast hills of wheat and long grasses. Colorful wildflowers grew up between the grass. It was so beautiful! A carpet of joy beneath the clear blue sky.

That's it! I thought as I ran out to the field. In tears, I looked up into the beautiful sky and said, "Lord, this is what I want to be for You … I want to bring You joy like these wildflowers are bringing me! I want to be Your little flower!" I reached down and picked a wildflower and took it up to my deck. As I soaked in my desire for Him, I wrote out a poem about how I wanted to be "His Little Flower" to bring the joy I was experiencing from these flowers back to Him. I wish I had a copy of that poem, but I don't.... It was put on the altar with the wildflower I picked. I didn't tell a soul. It was between me and Jesus.

Not long after returning from this retreat, I sat at my piano, alone in my grandma's old house. I was happy my two roommates were still gone at their jobs. I started playing random chords, singing prayers that came to my mind. As I worshiped, the Holy Spirit formed an image in my mind of a lit white candle.

It was so clear and peacefully glowing in the darkness surrounding it. Just then, words and a melody flooded my soul, "Candle Song." I had never had lyrics and melody come to me at the same time! It was such an encouragement.

♪♪♪ Candle Song ♪♪♪

Chorus: See the candle burning, deep inside your heart. I am here to warm you, make a brand-new start.

Verse 1: You are washed clean in My blood; know that I am in you and make a brand-new start. Keep your eyes upon Me, see My life within you. I am here to light your way, helping you through each day. (Chorus)

Verse 2: Know that I'll never leave you. Put your life in My hands, yes, I make all things new. Give me all your worries, rest in my light. I'll make everything all right. Have faith, you'll have a new sight. (Chorus)

Verse 3: I am the way, the truth, and the life. No one comes to the Father except through Me. If you abide in My Word, then you are My own, and you shall know the truth, and the truth shall make you free. (Chorus)

During the process of writing this book, I professionally recorded "Candle Song." It was fun to play the piano and sing this again. You can listen to it here: You can also find it on YouTube, Apple, Pandora, iTunes, and Amazon. Just search "Georgia Morris" (artist) or "Candle Song" (title).

The following year, when I was twenty, my sister Susie and her husband, Joe, invited me to their house for dinner. They had moved back to the Spokane area from Texas, to an area called Garden Springs. It didn't dawn on me until I started writing this, forty years later, that the name "Garden Springs" was so significant with what was about to happen.

They also invited a friend of ours, Chris Henton, whom I knew through a young-adult small group that he and I helped lead at St. Charles, the parish I grew up in. That evening, Chris brought his older brother, Mark. He was eleven years older than me, seemed kind, and was a Christian. It was evident to everyone that he and Chris were close. I'd met Mark once, about a year before this at a dinner a group of us went to. At the time, he'd had a girlfriend with him, and I didn't really talk to him that night.

After having dinner, my brother-in-law, Joe, asked if anyone wanted prayer.

No one said anything, so I chirped in, "Sure, I can always use prayer."

The four of them gathered around me to pray.

After a few minutes of quiet, Joe said, "Umm, I am wondering if I can share something I just saw so clearly in the Spirit, but I'm not sure what it means at all or if it'll mean anything to you, Georgia."

I asked him to please share.

He said, "I see a man like a Father holding a little girl on His lap, and He's saying repeatedly to her, 'My little flower. My little flower.' Does this mean anything at all to you, Georgia?"

This took my breath away! I had never shared with anyone about my retreat a whole year before this night with the poem and flower I left at the altar. Joe's vision was a gift of renewed acceptance from God Himself! My Father's mindfulness of me left me stunned. In awe, I realized that He saw me and heard me that day in the wildflower field. Just like at the Pacific Ocean, He confirmed His love to me again, recognizing me as His little flower in Garden Springs! I was overjoyed and flooded with peace.

Soon afterward, I drove home, pondering what just happened, full of thanksgiving and praise that God had forgiven me once again! He forgave all the mistakes I thought deep down had devastated my relationship with Him for good. Lamentations 3:22–23 (NASB) says, "The Lord's acts of mercy indeed do not end, for His compassions do not fail. They are new every morning; great is Your faithfulness." Truly the Lord is so good, and His mercies are new every morning, even when we don't deserve it.

So I drove home right after that amazing time, filled with awe, treasuring every second. I made it back to my house, and my two friends I lived with were not home. *Good.* I wanted to treasure this moment as long as I could in solitude and with such joy and gratitude!

For about fifteen minutes, I basked in the tangible love of my Father, worshiping Him in music and prayer. In the middle of pouring out thanksgiving from my soul, a knock came at my front door. If it had been one of my housemates, she would have just come right in. Who could this be?

I crossed the room and curiously opened the door. There stood Mark Henton from the barbecue. Mark? What was he doing here? He had never been at my home before; how did he even know where it was? Maybe I had forgotten something at Susie's, and she'd told him how to get here to return it.

His voice was calm and earnest. "Georgia, I have something I need to tell you."

This was bewildering for sure. "Okay." I hesitantly pulled the door open and stepped aside. "Come inside and have a seat."

We sat down and faced each other.

"Georgia, when Joe was telling you about the vision he had, the Lord was telling me something too. As he talked about the Father holding a little girl and saying, 'My little flower' over and over, the Holy Spirit revealed to me that it meant you would become my wife."

Disgust and dread and anger shot through my body. "*What?*" I almost spat the words. "*No!* You are wrong and know nothing of what it meant to me. Plus, I don't even know you!" God Himself had spoken to me, answering my prayer from a year ago, showing me again that He saw me and that I mattered to Him. No way was this stranger going to spoil that precious moment. "What Joe said was for *me*. I asked the Lord a year ago to make me like a flower that could bring joy to Him, and I never told anyone about it. No human being knew, and Joe's vision was a confirmation from the Lord."

Mark scrunched his face ever so slightly, probably wondering if he had gotten it wrong. "I don't know. It seemed very clear to me that God was saying He'd chosen you to be my wife. Will you at least pray about it? I think we should start getting to know each other."

"What about your girlfriend I met at the dinner last year?"

"We aren't together anymore. But you should know I have been married before. When I was seventeen, I got my girlfriend at the time pregnant. We were married for five years and have a son named Isaac. He's ten years old now. But that didn't work out either. My ex-wife has been remarried for the last three years, and the Lord has done a huge amount of healing in me. Just recently, I've been completely set free from her. I have so much peace, and I know in my heart that I can move on and remarry. That's why that vision tonight was so significant. Please pray about it and let me know if we can start seeing each other."

None of this made any sense to me. Why would God use a personal-to-me love confirmation to tell this man that I would be his wife? He was *eleven* years older than me. And I hadn't even had a passing thought of him, didn't know him at all! Could there be any truth to what he said? But I had given my life so completely to Jesus that I didn't want to miss out on what He wanted me to do … not again, even if I didn't understand it. So I agreed we could at least spend some time together.

CHAPTER EIGHT

Getting to Know Mark

Over the next six months or so we saw each other here and there, but I was very hesitant to be in any serious relationship. Mark owned and was also the chief mechanic for a snowmobile and Norton/Triumph motorcycle dealership shop. He had a very sweet personality and loved Jesus. But I was so confused. If the Lord was in this, I still wasn't sure. During my third year of college, I decided to take a day off school and my job at the dry cleaners to seek the Lord for an answer. I told the Lord, "I'm not leaving this room until I hear direction from You," and I knelt down next to my bed and began to pray and wait.

After several hours I had a very clear vision, so vivid, almost like a movie going on in my mind. I had only experienced this level of clarity in a vision once before when I was praying with Susie after returning from Sacramento when I was eighteen. Here's the vision:

There was the milk truck Lord of Love Community was about to purchase. And there was EWU. I only had one more year to complete a bachelor of arts degree (music specialist, K–12). The faces of many people in the community I was involved with appeared before me, and

I had so much joy, because I was finally set free from the guilt and shame of the sexual relationship I'd had with my boss at the dental lab. Healing and wholeness flooded me as I moved on from this dark time. Everything was going so well!

The scene changed, and a very narrow path appeared before me with only Mark facing me, standing there with his arms at his side, slightly open. He had no expression as he stood there. There was nothing beyond him except a narrow dirt path.

I then heard a voice in my mind so plainly say, "You can choose to stay on the path of the wide road that has many good opportunities happening for you, or you can choose this narrow path of marrying Mark. If you choose this path with Mark, you will suffer … but the joy you will receive in knowing Me will not be able to be compared with anything! You will know Me more fully than going the other way, and I will be with you."

The vision then ended. It absolutely took my breath away. I had no doubt that it was from God Himself because I had wanted the Lord to guide my life, above anything, and certainly above Mark, whom I hardly knew. It's a strange thing because it wasn't so much a physical or emotional attraction to him as much as I was convinced that God had brought him into my life. He was a sweet person and nice looking, owned a home and a successful business. He seemed stable in many ways. Overall, I just didn't want to miss the mark (*no pun intended*) if this was ordained by God. After that time of prayer, I knew God wanted me to marry him despite what others around me said. So I decided that I would say yes in faith, trusting this was the right thing to do. I believed with all my heart that it was.

Halfway through my twenty-first year, we were engaged. There was great conflict within me because my parents had a problem with it all. Dad said he thought Mark was a con artist, and Dad and Mom were both against this marriage. The weird thing is, not long before this, I had attended a Christian conference at the Spokane Coliseum, and someone preached about how we should and need to have our father's blessing to marry, if possible. I knew this and wanted to have my dad's blessing, but when I shared it with Mark, he said I shouldn't listen to my dad because he was deceived, being in the Catholic church. Mark and his brother had been raised Catholic, too, even attending St. Charles, the same parish we were in. Anyway, he showed me a Scripture that said, "Do not call anyone on earth 'father,' for you have one Father, and he is in heaven" (Matthew 23:9), and of course we grew up calling priests "father." It was all very confusing to me, but I started giving an ear to what he was saying. Through an emotional and spiritual battle, I succumbed to all this. I was a newly devoted Christian and hungered for living after the Word, applying what I read to my life, and being obedient in every way to the Holy Spirit. I read Scripture, prayed, and loved Jesus. Jesus was so real to me, like never before. He became my best friend again but this time as an adult. Those days I had made room for Him in my seat at elementary school had been so carefree. As an adult, I was now making harder decisions, and I didn't want to let Him down. Despite confusion, I chose to go the way of marrying Mark Henton on July 25, 1981.

As I write this now, over forty years later, I honestly cannot remember how he asked me to marry him. But I do remember that when my friends and sisters offered to drive me to the Finch Arboretum for the wedding rehearsal, I said no thanks. I really needed to drive myself. And I cried out so loudly all the way there for God to stop this wedding if I was wrong. It was turmoil, and yet I felt like it was the best thing to do to be closer to God.

I had just turned twenty-two the month before. Both of my parents walked me down the aisle at an outside wedding ceremony at the Finch Arboretum under the largest tree there. Some of my closest friends from the Lord of Love Community and the Gonzaga Friday-night chapel attended, and my family attended, even though most of them were hesitant and broken-hearted about my marrying Mark, especially my parents. But they knew I had made up my mind. It was a beautiful, sunny day. In writing this now, I cannot even recall where we had our reception.

But I do remember having a wonderful week in Victoria, British Columbia, for our honeymoon. We stayed in a nice hotel and visited the Butchart Gardens. The flowers there were so lovely! I was so happy and often thought, *I can't believe I'm married!* I determined to love Mark with all my heart. After that wonderful week, we drove back to Spokane.

Four or five weeks after the wedding, Mark wanted to take me on an extended camping trip. Camping sounded fine to me. I had camped with my family of ten in tent trailers or trailers we rented and pulled with our station wagons. But Mark and I didn't take a tent. Even though I had never camped in the open air, Mark really wanted to fish and camp, so with some hesitancy, I went along with it. We borrowed some of his dad's strong fishing poles for salmon fishing and his dad's small metal fishing boat with a large motor. We headed to the beach at Neah Bay, Washington. I had never been there before, but he had been there many times to fish in the ocean with his dad and brothers for salmon.

When we got to Neah Bay, we set up camp. I'm not sure what I expected, but I really didn't know we'd be right outside on the beach with nothing over our heads. The two of us carried the metal boat out to sea over the giant waves from the beach. After fighting the waves and getting into the boat, things became somewhat smooth. We balanced ourselves with our fishing poles ready! I had fished at lakes in small boats or off a dock with my dad and brothers and sisters but never in an ocean.

Once again, I was hesitant about how dangerous this risk was. And I was learning that Mark was a very determined person. When he wanted to do something, he did it, despite any risk. And he ignored my expressing how I felt—afraid!

I was trying to not let it all worry me. Suddenly, I felt sick, very nauseated every time a wave came and rocked the boat. "Mark, can we please stop fishing for a time and go to the beach? I'm really craving a milkshake." There was a small café close by our campsite that had fresh huckleberry homemade shakes. "I am not feeling well. Every time the boat rocks, I feel queasy."

"Sure, we can stop just as soon as we catch something!"

He wasn't going to stop until we caught a fish. So I began to quietly pray, *begging* the Lord to let him catch a fish! "Please Lord … I need to stop this fishing, and he won't unless he gets one on the line."

With each wave, I grew more and more nauseated … then in an instant, *my* fishing pole went down with a jerk! I held on with all my might and had to let Mark help, or I would have dropped it in the water. We both hung on together as the fish went under our little boat and the tip of the pole bent all the way down to the water. It almost tipped us over, so we also had to balance all that. It was quite a scene. Together, we pulled in a huge salmon that was about two-thirds my height! We then took it over to that little store that had the huckleberry shakes.

The people that owned the store were so nice and measured the salmon we caught and took my picture with it. It was about forty-six inches from head to tail. As I held it vertically from the ground, it came to above my waist, almost to my shoulders, and it was also about a foot wide in the widest part. It was so exciting! Mostly I was thrilled that God answered my prayer and also gave us food to live on for a couple of weeks. These people were really sweet and cleaned the fish and cut it up for us. They even put some in baggies and said they would freeze it for us until we went back to Spokane.

They had a few wooden booths in the café part, and we decided to sit down in one while we waited for them to clean our fish. Mark asked me what I wanted to eat. All I craved was that homemade huckleberry milkshake! It was so delicious, with fresh-picked local huckleberries, and my shakiness subsided for a bit after drinking this. I think we had a sandwich as well. We then took some of the cleaned fish that was cut up in pieces and cooked the salmon on a rack Mark found from a deserted refrigerator that had been tossed on the side of the road. We created a roaring fire in the pits they had on the beach with sticks we collected. It was quite an adventure, sleeping on the beach under the stars, and was very frightening to me, maybe a little fun, but I kept praying and trusting that the Lord was protecting us. Mark was fearless, and I tried to be, staring up at the stars. How different we were. As the stars twinkled and "sang together," it began to be fun. I must admit, though, that I felt a lot more secure in Victoria inside a hotel!

On one beautiful sunny day, we were walking together down the beach, and Mark became very quiet. The waves crashed gently on the beach, a seagull flew overhead, and a sand crab scurried away. What could be bothering him on such an idyllic day?

"Mark … are you all right?"

The only answer was the sound of the waves. How odd. His head hung low, and there was a great sense of heaviness about him. We kept walking in silence for a good amount of time. "Did I say or do anything to offend you?"

"No."

Silence.

We'd already walked quite a long distance without talking. I stopped. He kept walking with his head hanging down. He must have wanted to be alone. He'd gotten pretty far away from me when an eerie feeling swept through me. Perhaps he was thinking of his ex-wife and ten-year-old son. There was no way to know unless I asked him.

I ran to catch up with him. "Mark! Are you thinking of your ex-wife and Isaac?"

He didn't even glance my way. "Yes."

I froze as he strolled on ahead. My heart fractured! It had completely been his as I committed myself wholly to him as his new wife, and he was my husband. Betrayal and pain wrecked my soul like a hurricane. He had told me before we got married that he was so free from them. What had happened? Why was he thinking of them now when he was on *our* honeymoon! What could I say to that? What could I do? Slowly, I willed my legs into motion and returned to our campsite—alone.

CHAPTER NINE

A Season of Anticipation

When we returned from our extended honeymoon to our house in Spokane that he owned before we were married, I continued to feel queasy and went to the doctor. We found out that I was pregnant with our first baby. I was thrilled! Mark was too! My joyful attitude was a miracle, since after growing up in the middle of a large family, I had determined I would not ever have children. Things sure changed, and looking back, I'm so happy they did! I love my four children and seven grandchildren so very much, beyond words. My wife and mother instincts kicked in, and I was having so much fun realizing I was married and now pregnant, too!

At some point, soon into our marriage, Mark told me I had to quit school. I've never understood why, when I was so close to being finished. I was in my last year for my bachelor's degree in music. But he was serious. Even though I didn't understand it, I submitted. I also had to sell the piano I had grown up with. But I consoled myself with knowing Mark had a piano in his home I could play. I was fine about being free to be home.

Not long after this, I discovered that Mark was writing checks to his ex-wife every month. When I asked why he was writing them, he got really upset. I finally found out the money was beyond the child support he paid; it was alimony, which was supposed to have stopped when she remarried. In general, he wouldn't let me know what money we had, and it was always hard for me to ask for money or spend for groceries. Yet he paid her. I couldn't help but say something to him. It wasn't long after that he stopped writing her checks. After Mark stopped paying her, she told him thank you, because the money he'd given her had helped them buy their boat. She and her husband were both teachers at a high school.

I would see her sometimes when she was picking up or dropping off Isaac when he visited with us. Once when she was picking him up, we had a brief conversation on the front porch. "Don't be a doormat," she said. That stuck in my head for some time, especially when things got worse.

As the little life grew inside my womb, the thought of having my own baby infused my heart with overwhelming joy! I was going to have a baby … wow! Would the baby be a daughter or a son? It didn't matter, he or she would be a new little life for me to cherish. I began to feel more settled about everything. Mark continued working at the motorcycle shop. Things seemed to be going well. I was content to prepare the nursery. Sometimes we would go visit my parents for dinner or do things with family, mine and his dad and stepmother as well.

In the winter, Mark continued working as the shop's sole mechanic and continued selling snowmobiles. He was very skilled as a mechanic and a businessman. As I shared earlier, one of the creative outlets I had for many years was making those decoupaged wooden plaques for people with poems I found or made up myself. I decided to make a very large decoupaged poster for Mark while he was at the shop. Over the course of many days, I selected each item to include, pouring my whole heart into it. There were beautiful pictures, including some of us as bride and groom, nature scenes, beaches, and even a salmon! I painstakingly cut hearts and wrote messages that expressed my love, emotions of gratitude, and romance for him, which was growing. My soul abounded with anticipation at the thought of giving it to him. I wanted to be the best wife I could, and I sincerely put my all into this sentimental project. When I finally finished it, I was so elated and couldn't wait to see his expression when he received it.

When he got home one night from work, I gave it to him with a big grin.

He looked at it, gave a smirk, and kind of laughed. "What's this? I don't want this." And he threw it aside.

Once again, I felt absolutely crushed. He had taken my heart, trampled it, and thrown it aside as if it were trash. It became extremely hard to share any of my emotions with him after that. The feelings of love and elation at being married to him were being replaced by feelings of being trapped. Feelings of sadness overwhelmed me.

I would sometimes play the piano and worship with singing as I played. It wasn't very often, but he came to me once and said, "You shouldn't be playing."

I pushed down the confusion and annoyance. "Why?"

"Playing the piano is an idol to you."

Now this was really strange! I could hardly get myself to sit and play at all, so I certainly knew it was not an "idol" to me.

I just want to add a side note for those who may be wondering what this means. I know many friends and acquaintances of different beliefs and cultures. In the Christian faith, we believe God gave us His inspired Word in the Bible as our guide. In the Old Testament, the Ten Commandments were given to us through Moses. The first one in Exodus 20:3 says, "You shall have no other gods before me." To be clear, when Mark said this to me, I knew I wasn't putting (worshiping) the piano over God. This seemed ridiculous to me, but I knew he meant it and that was his perspective. I had to honor that, even though I didn't bear witness to it at all.

Things continued on with him controlling me more and more. This really caused me to plunge into God and come to know and rely upon Him as my very best friend even more. My heart ached; my only sources of joy were singing, praying, and anticipating the birth of this new life within me. I often sang the song "Bless the Lord, Oh My Soul" so full of joy and expectation, placing my hand on my belly and thinking of the baby being formed in me … and all that is within me. I sang a lot! I've since learned that your baby inside can hear sounds, and music in particular has an effect. When I worshiped or played music, I felt peace within myself but I also knew it was a benefit to my baby. More and more, I turned inward because that's where I felt safest. I had to guard my heart from being trampled on, emotionally or spiritually, anymore.

There was one time when I was about eight months pregnant that Mark pushed me down. I fell on the living room carpet. He was mad at something, and I still don't know what it was. Could it be because I was softly playing the piano while he was in another room? At the time, it shocked me. We didn't even really fight or argue, and this behavior came out of nowhere. Even worse, he laughed about it and refused to help me up. It was the weirdest thing and so hurtful. After that, I didn't play piano when he was at home.

I knew he had a lot of hurt and rage from past hurts, but I didn't know what or why. He never talked about them. Confusion set in again, and I didn't have anyone to talk to about it all. Shortly after this, while Mark was at work, I drove down to the Bowl and Pitcher, which is an area on the Spokane River in Riverside State Park where there are huge boulders, one that looks like a bowl and one that looks like a pitcher. It's a beautiful area for picnics and camping. There are many trails and a suspended bridge that people like to jump on to make it bounce up and down. As I walked across the bridge, everything seemed to be closing in on me. A loud thought came to me. *Why don't you just jump off and end all this misery?*

Wow! I was stunned at this very real and dark feeling that accompanied the voice in my mind. Nothing like this had ever happened to me before. I had to shake myself out of this dark cloud quickly and call out to Jesus. I immediately felt peace when I called for Jesus to help, and I knew that the voice in my mind was the devil. I came against that voice with a vengeance, and such great faith came up from within me. In fact, all this led to praise, joy, and thanksgiving for the precious life within me! That very moment became an anchor for my soul and would bring me strength when I was down. Carrying this baby inside me gave me hope and the desire to worship with deep joy from within. It was a privilege to be pregnant, and I was so thankful for this little life within me! The hope I had outdid any dark voices that tried to destroy me or bring me down. As I look back, I realize that as a new life was being formed within me, I was also in my own amniotic sac or chrysalis. And Satan was working hard to destroy my life and my son's life before he was even born.

Thank You, Lord, for Your divine ways, for caring for us and letting us know how mindful You are of us. Truly, Your love never fails! I knew in that moment of such torment that when I had lifted my eyes to You, You were there to help me and cause me to see that I had more to live for than Mark.... You were creating new life in me to care for in the midst of my trouble. And I would do everything in my power to protect it!

Psalm 46:1 says, "God is our refuge and strength, an ever-present help in trouble." He became that to me more and more as I relied upon Him and remembered to call out to Him for help instead of relying on my own strength, which began to quickly fade.

I returned home and continued with daily life. I was becoming quite the homemaker, diving into cooking and learning how to can fruits. The memories of cooking for my reassuring dad were becoming far away as I became my own chef without the encouragement of Mark. But I loved cooking, and I also planted a garden and became very domesticated. Overall, I was glad I could be at home.

CHAPTER TEN

From Bad to Worse

For the first few years of our marriage, Mark and I attended church together. The people of the church became my family and my spiritual lifeline through the years I was with him. There I met our good friend Nancy. She graciously threw me a big baby shower at her house, and Mark even allowed my family to attend.

On April 23, 1982, our precious baby was born. A boy! We named him Jeremiah "Jeremy" Paul. What a little package of joy he was! Both my parents and our good friend Nancy were able to be with us at his birth. It was glorious when he came into the world after twenty-four hours of extremely hard labor.

I was so very thankful to be able to have my parents at the birth, especially since Mark had become closed off to communicating or spending any time with them. I was shocked when he said they could be there. My dad had never been allowed to be with my mom when she birthed the nine of us. This was a huge blessing!

I was able to nurse Jeremy for about eight months, and I wish it could have been longer, but when he was around seven months old, I started feeling very weak every time he nursed. We soon discovered the reason. I was pregnant again! Was it a beautiful girl this time? Or was it another adorable little boy? We loved waiting for the surprise to find out.

One night, when Jeremy was almost one year old, and I was about four months pregnant, Mark decided that he wanted to take Jeremy on his shoulders to walk around outside in the backyard. It was nine o'clock and dark. Usually Jeremy was already in bed but not that night.

I tried to stop him. "Mark, you can't take him outside in the dark and cold! It's way past his bedtime. He needs to go to bed!"

He turned on me, reached for my throat, then pushed me away, picked up Jeremy and proceeded to go outside. That particular night, I called friends for advice and they encouraged me to call 911. The 911 operator gave me a mental health hotline to call. My friends came over, and at that time, Mark had come back inside. Jeremy was put to bed and things calmed down. This was just an example of incidents that became more regular.

There were some very scary times during my second pregnancy, because about seven months along, the doctor discovered the placenta was pulling away from the uterus. He said there was a fifty-fifty chance of the baby's survival. This could all heal with bedrest, but without it, I would lose the baby, so I did as much bedrest as I could with a toddler. But once again, I had friends who came over, especially Nancy, who was such a blessing and extremely helpful! Mark didn't seem to have a problem with her. I know my own family would have been there in a heartbeat if Mark had allowed it, but instead, I was receiving help from very close friends, of which I am forever grateful.

Our second little bundle of joy was born on July 29, 1983. "It's a boy!" I heard the doctor say. We were elated! When I first held him, impressions flooded my heart from my recent study through the book in the Bible called Joel. *Joel* seemed so appropriate for him. Mark agreed and liked the name. Little did I know then that later in his life Joel Nathaniel would live up to his name and become a pastor and one who has a prophetic call on his life. He is not afraid to speak truth and never has been. When he was four years old, we visited a Christmas service at a church in Spokane. They had live animals, and I'll always remember how he tapped me on my arm and begged to go down at the end of the service when they opened up prayer for those who wanted to come to God. He recalls even today that that was the day he gave his heart to Christ. He has continued to live dedicated to God and, now, to his precious family as well. He has a heart and burden for people to know the Lord. He majored in music at a Bible school and served as a worship pastor, youth pastor, and for the past ten years, a senior pastor. It's been such a blessing to watch his growth and maturity, as a husband and as a father to our two wonderful grandsons who are the oldest of our seven now!

Jeremy and Joel are only fifteen months apart. It was a very busy time. Before Joel learned to walk or talk, his face shined with happiness. Baby Joel just loved looking up at us with big smiles. His big brother Jeremy especially entertained him really well! Joel giggled and smiled a lot and was a super happy baby, bringing us tremendous joy!

On one occasion, I was coming back from getting groceries with Mom, a rare moment of being with her. Mark was probably at work. She asked if we were planning to have any more children.

Almost before thinking it, I said, "Mom, I feel like I will someday have a little girl, but it won't be with Mark. I'm not sure what that means. I don't ever plan on leaving him."

Around this time, my friend Cliff, who I used to sing at weddings with, gave me his old guitar. I taught myself to play chords so I could sing with an instrument and played when Mark was at work so he wouldn't complain. My prayer life and worshiping with guitar and songs grew as things became even more difficult.

The next major blow was when Mark said I couldn't have any time or communication with my family. I was so close to my parents and siblings, but he said I must choose between him and them. He couldn't tell me why. The several times we'd gone over to their house for dinner, he always seemed happy. They accepted him, and now, for some reason, he wanted to cut me off from all ties with them. I believe now he had jealousy, as later I learned more about his upbringing. Even when I would see my mom and dad at Safeway, I'd have to ignore them, changing aisles to avoid them. It hurt them so much and me as well. We only lived about two to three miles from them, but it seemed like a thousand. I was so sad, yet I kept thinking I needed to submit to my husband, no matter the cost. And I had a hope that in doing this, he might change.

When Mark was home, I never knew how he would be. Sometimes he would play with the kids and be helpful. Other times, he criticized me a lot. For example, one time we were praying together, just normal, nothing weird, and he interrupted me and said, "That's not the Holy Spirit" as he got up and walked away. Random things like that happened more often, and he became very mean. I never knew what mood he would be in. Often, what he was saying wouldn't make much sense at all.

It became common for Mark to twist everything I said. It was emotionally exhausting and tormenting. The thoughts came, *am I crazy?* I'd have to remind myself it was not *me*, this was him. I knew what I meant … the battle of the mind was constant. Reasoning with him got me nowhere. He definitely was sick, but his behavior just seemed more like manipulation. Sometimes it felt like I could help, but I would always realize I couldn't. The only thing I could do was to care for and love him, but it was very difficult. Sometimes I just wanted to scream! As time went on, I didn't see him getting better but getting worse, and that pain was horrific.

He began saying such harsh words that cut to my core. Always putting me down. Always making me feel like I was a liar. Anger built up in me, and one time, I tried to hit him as hard as I could … but pulled back with a hard jerk because I knew it wasn't right. My arm came completely out of the socket. It was such grueling pain! My body was breaking down because of the daily stress. Mark actually told me to relax, took my arm, and as he stretched it, it popped back into the socket. Weird that he helped, looking back at how harsh he had been moments before that happened. But I'm so glad he did! And I never *tried* to hit him again, that's for sure.

I was so desperate and knew something had to change. A trusted couple who were leaders in our church said I could move in with them for a time. So when Joel was three weeks old, and Jeremy was sixteen months old, I took the boys and we moved into their place.

Baby Joel (two mo.) and Jeremy (seventeen mo.) at Tim's

It was a tremendous blessing to see a married couple that treated each other so lovingly. And it was a peaceful place. I realized then how dark and lonely it was where I was living and how much bondage the boys and I were really in.

Mark and I had marriage counseling while I was there. He came several times and a couple of the elders of our church encouraged Mark to not put pressure on himself to be some great man of God. All the Lord wanted him to do was to love Him and love his wife and kids. They were quite encouraging to both of us.

After several weeks of living there, I was praying out in their garden in the backyard, and I felt a clear urge to go back home, as hard as this would be. I had absolutely no desire ... but I was reminded of Jesus when He was in the garden and prayed "Not *my* will, but yours be done" after He asked and begged the Father to take this cup from Him (see Luke 22:42 and Mark 14:36). I was also reminded of the vision I had of the narrow path where there would be suffering, but that if I went that way (marrying Mark), I would know the intimacy of Christ so much more. This was proving itself daily. I had just turned twenty-four a few months before, and Mark was thirty-five. In the few years we'd been together, my relationship with Jesus had matured far beyond what I ever expected, and I never realized how in my weakness and desperation, reliance on God and not myself caused me to know Him so much more. And He truly became my best friend. I definitely knew going home was not going to be an easy road. But I also realized I made the choice to marry Mark. So ... I decided to go back home. I called Mark at work to let him know the boys and I were coming back home, and he seemed excited.

The next day, we moved back home. I put the kids down for naps and decided to make a very nice dinner for Mark and myself. The time he normally got home came and went, and I tried to keep the food warm. Mark was so unpredictable, there was no way to know what was going on. It was such a cold autumn day. What could he be doing? He was usually pretty prompt about getting home right after work. More time passed, and I got a call.

"Ma'am, this is Officer Johnson. Do you know Mark Henton?"

"Yes, sir. He is my husband." Fear spiraled around my heart and threatened to squeeze. "Is he alright?"

"Well, he's alive and appears to be okay, but he won't open his eyes, and he's unresponsive. We found him face down on the concrete floor of his shop. The man who owns the gas station next door saw his lights still on past closing time and thought that was unusual. He went over to check, found Mr. Henton on the floor, and called 911. They transported him to Holy Family Emergency. We would like you to come here and see if you can get him to respond."

The fear that had threatened my soul turned to numbness. I called some friends, who came over to be with the boys. Then I contacted the church leader I had just stayed with, Tim, and asked if he would meet me at the ER.

When I got there, Tim's presence immediately brought a sense of security. He was a retired professional football player, and his size and strength felt like added protection as we walked into the unknown. We were met by a couple of doctors, medical professionals, and the nurse who first helped Mark when the ambulance brought him. Tim and I proceeded to go into Mark's room with her. It was terrifying to see him hooked up to tubes of oxygen, eyes closed, and not responsive.

One of the attendants approached me. "Mrs. Henton, do you know if Mr. Henton has ever taken any drugs or drank alcohol?"

"No. I don't think he has. Not since I married him, for sure, and he always talked about hating them."

"We aren't quite sure what happened. The police didn't find any evidence of a break-in, and it doesn't look like anyone tried to hurt him." He seemed as bewildered as I was.

"Just last night I talked to him to tell him the boys and I were coming home today. We've been gone for several weeks. He sounded very excited to know we were coming home."

"Well, his vitals are all within normal range, and we can't see any reason why he wouldn't be able to wake up and talk with us. But he won't respond to any of the hospital staff. Will you please talk to him and see if he will respond to you?"

I moved to his bedside. With a sweet and sincere voice, I said, "Mark … honey, the boys and I are so excited for you to come home. I love you. They do too. I made a delicious dinner for us tonight. We are glad to come back home and be with you. I have great hope that things are going to be better."

No response.

"Mark, can you tell me what happened?"

Still no response.

"What's wrong? I am sorry for leaving. But I felt I had to at the time. Hopefully we can start fresh, with the support of others."

No response.

"Mark, can you hear me?" It was a losing battle. There was no response at all! His eyes remained closed, and he looked dead but was breathing.

Tim stepped up behind me. Tapping me on the shoulder, he whispered, "Georgia, can I try?"

I nodded my head. Sadness overwhelmed me, and my emotions were whipping into a whirlwind. As I stared at Mark's lifeless form, a very large hand dropped upon his chest.

Mark jerked and opened his eyes, then quickly shut them. He had been faking his "catatonic" state the whole time!

Tim's surprise attempt hadn't hurt Mark but had shocked him out of his charade.

When we left the room, the nurse commented to me and to the doctors that in all her thirty-five-plus years of working with catatonic patients, he was the first to put forth an effort to help her get his leather jacket off! She was quite amused by it, and from there, my memory is blank as far as that night. He didn't come home right away. I believe he was put in a psychiatric ward for some observation for a time. But this was the beginning of the "from bad to worse," which would continue for many more years.

Bear with me, please, because these memories ahead have some vivid moments. Some are very joyful with my boys and the Lord's amazing presence, and others are gut-wrenching. The time frame is right, but the order of what I write may be a bit scattered. I will do my best with the following years.

CHAPTER ELEVEN

Learning to Yield

So many awful things come to me now as I look back on the past years, but I cannot deny that those bruised years were also ones that formed my own character, my faith in God's real presence, and the blessings of my two boys. Evil has been and will always be overcome by good. Romans 12:21 says, "Do not be overcome by evil, but overcome evil with good."

After the hospital incident, I believe Mark was taken to Eastern State Hospital for two to four weeks for assessment and to determine which meds would work best. He was diagnosed with manic depression. I was considered his legal guardian at that time, and it was the law that anyone who was competent could and should call mental health services for someone else who was considered or diagnosed not competent. Basically, he was an involuntary patient, and I was responsible for calling for help because he wouldn't do it for himself. So when he was discharged from Eastern, I had the responsibility of picking him up.

He seemed relieved and happy to be out of there and reunited with the kids and me. This may have lasted a few weeks to a few months, but then there would be difficult times when I would have to call mental health services again. When they sent meds home with him, he wouldn't take them, and I couldn't make him. There was a real pattern developing where he would seem fine for a while, and then he would spiral downward. He was getting worse.

I don't think he ever was balanced, especially after that time in the shop of faking a coma. Even though the hospital diagnosed him with manic depression, years later, his diagnosis changed to schizophrenia. There were real mental problems, but all the medical professionals confirmed that he was manipulative and there must have been some trauma in his past. They may have given him some counseling in the hospital, but if they did, I never knew about it. He would be given drugs to calm him down and then released back to me and the kids at home. There wasn't ever any follow-up, at least not that Mark would allow or acknowledge. So I took it upon myself to begin asking him questions about his past. We had never really talked about this when we were engaged. It had just been surface information. It could have been greatly beneficial to our marriage if I had learned more about Mark before I entered into a serious relationship with him and especially before agreeing to marry him. Although, at the time of our engagement, there were no signs of his problems. He seemed stable.

In my pursuit to find out what Mark's hurts were from his past, I learned for the first time that his mom, whose name was Helen, committed suicide after she and his dad divorced. He and his brother Chris found her reaching for the phone in the home they grew up in. He described how awful that was.

And as a little boy, he remembered standing between his mom and dad as they yelled at each other. She would throw silverware and sometimes vegetable cans, yelling over and over to his dad, "You don't love me."

Mark's dad, Ben, had been a widower before he married Helen and already had three boys. He had lost his first wife, who was also named Helen, to leukemia. After he married his second Helen, Mark was born, and two years later, his brother was born. So now Mark's mom was raising five boys, three of them stepsons. Ben would work hard all day as a sheet metal worker and then on weekends go build their lake cabin. She was left alone a lot (according to what Mark said) with all five boys. As you can see, the family upbringing was unstable and chaotic. I was glad he opened up to me about his past.

As I got to know Ben more, he seemed like a great, caring man. He was retired when I knew him and remarried to a third Helen. Yes, another Helen! She was a sweet and wise person. We all loved her, and the kids called her Grandma. She and Ben square danced together, and we would go watch them and sometimes participate a little at the Spokane Valley Grange. They would come over for Christmas, and we would go to visit them at their home. The boys loved spending days watching Grandpa Ben work in his barn, creating sheet metal toys and yard decor and wooden birdhouses and even a wooden go-cart! He also took them on small rides on his motorcycle around the backyard. He was quite the craftsman! Then it was time to go inside to Grandma's kitchen and have her home-baked cookies or soup and sandwiches before leaving for home.

Grandpa Ben and Jeremy on the motorcycle

These favorite times made happy memories, but suddenly Mark would not allow his parents into our home. I continued a relationship with Ben and Helen, but it was so sad to see them at our door with gifts for the kids only to have to turn them away because Mark said he didn't want to see them. It caught all of us off guard. He was doing the same thing to them as he did to my parents and family. I know they were somewhat understanding about it later on, but initially it was grueling. Hearts were broken, and he didn't seem to care at all. I think that was the hardest thing. He didn't seem to care, but we all did.

Then things got to the point that Mark refused to eat. I tried to coax him, and he would take a spoonful when I fed him, but he wouldn't eat on his own. So now I had two babies to feed, and it felt like I had a third with him. I was his nurse really, not his wife. The hardest thing wasn't feeding him but the smirk he gave me afterward, as food dribbled down his chin. I would try everything to love him, from speaking sweetly and kindly to being firm and stressing how much we needed him. He needed to take care of himself, and he would only get better if he could know that and do it. But I was not successful with anything I said or did really.

I began praying in the bathroom with the door locked when the boys were asleep a lot of the time. That became my safe hiding place, and the Lord always gave me His strength and peace as I prayed and read the Bible, sitting on the bathroom floor lined with towels. I would give the boys bath time, play and sing songs, have a great time laughing, then put them to bed after singing a lullaby and cuddles. Then I'd go back into the bathroom and have my quiet time. I read a lot of the Psalms. They helped put me in touch with my own emotions. Here are several examples of psalms that gave me strength and peace. Psalm 63:7–8 says, "Because you are my help, I sing in the shadow of your wings. I cling to you; your right hand upholds me." Another, Psalm 25:15, says, "My eyes are ever on the Lord, for only he will release my feet from the snare." And Psalm 119:105: "Your word is a lamp for my feet, a light on my path."

I was holding up so much, trying to be a peaceful mom and loving wife, but inside I was crumbling. This was my haven. The presence of the Lord meeting me when I cried out to Him for help gave me a deep sense of security. I was so lonely but not alone. Reading the Bible gave me great comfort. Prayers would often come to me that turned into songs. Here is one:

♫ Yield (1985) ♫

Verse 1: When I yield to Your Spirit, oh Lord, what to me seems so painful and rough becomes glorious inside of faith, knowing that as I give, I'm giving to You.

Chorus: Mighty God, I yield my life. Seal me in Your precious way. Lead me, Lord, I need You. Let me rest in Your bosom today.

Verse 2: I wait, my soul waits for You Lord, and in Your Word do I hope. Bring me into Your fullness, O God. Let it be to me according to Your will. (Chorus)

After writing this book, in November 2023, I professionally recorded "Yield" using the original guitar I played in 1985 when I wrote it. You can listen to it at

You can also search Georgia Morris as artist on iTunes, YouTube, Apple, Pandora, and Amazon. The title is "Yield."

*Me playing the original guitar I used when first inspired
to write the song, recorded in 2023*

Worship brought peace to my heart. I decided to do it more, not just hidden away in the bathroom but also with the boys! Jeremy and Joel would jump up and down with me as we sang together and danced around! I still have a cassette tape of their little voices at ages three and four singing together with me "King of Kings," "His Name Is Jesus," and "What a Mighty God We Serve." 🙌 The Holy Spirit and joy began ruling our home more than any depression or dark spirit. We had a constant need to worship for my peace and sanity and their joy too. Through it all, the Lord really protected us. I made sure we went to church and to different friends' homes for dinner and fellowship, and we played in lots of parks. We'd also go out to Green Bluff, a cherry orchard a few miles outside of Spokane, and pick cherries. The boys helped pit them with the fun cherry pitter that we still have. And it works!

I also planted a big garden in our backyard, and the boys helped me. All of it was such therapy for us. Singing became a way of life everywhere we went. The boys would help shovel snow (mostly play in it), play

Legos and games, and we'd sing and dance. And I'd read lots of books, especially Bible stories.

Joel (age three) and Jeremy (age four) shoveling at home on Glass St., 1985/Supermen! 1987

CHAPTER TWELVE

Song in the Night

I bought lots of seeds, and we decided to try planting herbs, veggies, fruits (cantaloupe and watermelon didn't grow so well, but strawberries did!), and some pumpkins. I was so surprised when about one hundred pumpkins overtook our backyard. It was really fun! Of course, the boys loved playing in the dirt with their little shovels and trucks, and then the wading pool was always a fun way to rinse off! At some point, I learned that "Georgia" means "farmer"! I was living up to my name without realizing it.

Outside of our backyard fence, there was an area of dirt where I decided to plant some Zinnia flower seeds. There was a neighbor who had some river dirt they were not using, so I asked if I could have some of it. Amazingly, Mark helped me bring the dirt across the street, making several trips. I mixed it in with the dirt that was there already and planted Zinnia seeds about two inches apart like it said, placing a few in each hole. These tiny seeds produced flowers that were six feet tall! I was truly dumbfounded, and I even had neighbors stopping by to ask how they got so big. They wondered where I bought the plant starts, and I told them they were seeds from a package I bought from Northwest Seed & Pet. I had never planted anything like this before. When I was growing up, I'd help with planting petunias, but they were already six-inch starts.

As I was planting seeds, the Lord revealed many insights into this season of life. This was a precious time in which the Lord Himself was planting seeds of love and light in the boys and me. He was sowing in my character more of a need for Him than I had ever had. I had to cling to Him for my own sanity. During these times of daily routine, I continually received fresh lessons from God and shared them on a simple level with my boys, teaching them about the Lord and His ways. I learned to look to the Lord as my husband and decided that He could and would be my strength, no matter what.

As I pulled weeds one day, I realized that each kind of plant, whether it be vegetables (beans, carrots, peas) or fruits (strawberries) had a weed with an appearance very similar to the real plant. The Lord spoke to me clearly that Satan tries to copy God, but he isn't the real deal. Weeds destroy life, while true plants nourish. And the weeds try to hide and strangle out the true plant so it can't produce the nourishment it is meant to give others. Jesus said in John 10:10, "The thief comes only to steal and kill and destroy; I have come that they may have life, and have it to the full." My eyes became more open to the spiritual battle going on for our lives. Both boys had threats during my pregnancies, and my own life was threatened many times, strangling being one. But I also was seeing that Mark was being used by a spiritual power, and I was desperate to fight against the evil that plagued him.

On several occasions, he was gone for extended periods of time to the Sacred Heart psychiatric ward or Eastern State Hospital. Within five or so years, I had to call mental health many times. Each time I called, they would take him away, involuntarily, which was always so hard to watch as he struggled. Two or three men would try to ask him to walk out on his own, but he'd resist and physically fight them. They would finally have to force him down on a gurney, strapping down his arms and legs and body as they took him out the door. It was gut-wrenching to watch. And seeing our neighbors peer outside their windows at the charades, never saying anything but knowing something horrible was going on, was really sad.

Every time, I was able to protect the boys from seeing Mark being taken away. It was really hard to plan. But I did have wonderful friends who helped out when I asked. One was Cliff, who gave me the guitar. He lived with another single guy named Wes. Cliff and Wes would sometimes take the boys sledding at Mount Spokane or take them to parks to play when mental health services visited our home. They also helped me out with mowing our big yard, and lots of times, they would play Legos and games with the boys to give me some time to myself.

I'd have to make trips out to the state psychiatric hospital to take his clothing. Sometimes they said I couldn't see him because he was in a confined place to keep others safe from him harming them. Or I'd be escorted into a room where he was drugged up like a zombie (they said they were in the process of finding a balance and what meds would help). He didn't recognize me.

Usually, after he was released, he was dropped off at the Otis hotel, which was a horrible place, but it was an in-between place before coming home that he had to go to. I would have to pick him up. A few times I had to take the boys with me … it was so hard!

Yes, Mark had problems, and it was evident he had no peace. He was tormented and took out his own frustrations on us, especially me. The battle was beyond me, but understanding it helped to strengthen me and to give me the ability to forgive him. Mark was sick, and it was hard to see that clearly at the time, because he would smirk and act like he knew what he was doing. But I had to *continually* forgive him. Often many times in one day. Forgiveness sets the prisoners free, and if I held on to unforgiveness and anger, I was a slave myself to bondage. Liberty was in my blood, yes, but true liberty comes through the blood Jesus shed for us all. He made a way for us to experience true healing when we forgive others. It makes me think of the forgiveness He gave to the thief next to Him who was dying, who said, "Jesus, remember me when you come into your kingdom." Jesus answered him, "Truly I tell you, today you will be with me in paradise" (Luke 23:42–43). Just like that, mercy and forgiveness were given to the man who recognized he was unworthy and that Jesus had done nothing wrong.

I prayed for God to give me a heart to forgive Mark. Even though forgiveness hasn't happened overnight, I can honestly say now I forgive Mark completely and can actually pray and talk with him freely. He is not my responsibility to save or change, and I have grown in that understanding, realizing how my own feelings and heart have been affected by his misery. It was and has been a process of being cut off from the torment in my own soul, and that is so difficult when you are married or emotionally connected to someone whom you deeply care for. Emotional ties are normal, but when they are destructive, a cut is necessary.

My gratitude is huge even now, for my song in the night is stronger than evil and breaks the hold darkness has on a life, whatever the trials may be. Worship sets a heart free and is the expression of true neediness, forgiveness, surrender, and joy. Even recently, I was able to visit Mark in the group home he lives in, and we sang together! He is in a place of good care and loves to sing. It dawned on me that the very one who tried to quench my singing now lives daily with singing, always wanting to share a song on his heart with anyone who will listen. He prays for each of our family, including my husband, Wes, and me and all our children, grandchildren, and in-laws. It gives me a new song in my heart. Things have been redeemed, hearts have been healed, and we await more fullness. But while on this earth, our hearts rejoice in the newness and freedom there is in knowing Christ and serving Him.

The motorcycle shop sat empty for over a year and an extremely cold winter. There was no income at all. I was willing to go to work, but Mark wouldn't let me. I made cornmeal muffins, eating vegetables I had frozen and fruits I had canned. The boys and I were invited to eat dinner many times with families from our church. But we were running out of money. We were getting desperate!

Over those years, the stress of surviving continued to take a toll on my body. My shoulders came out of their sockets, twice more on each side. It was so painful. One of the times I was nursing Joel, the other arm came out unexpectedly as I lay on my side on our bed. I almost dropped him to the floor but caught him just in the nick of time. I also remember staying overnight with friends on a pullout sofa bed, and I turned over in the morning, and my arm came out of the socket. The boys were there peacefully watching cartoons with my friend's kids, and I started screaming uncontrollably and writhing in pain. My friend called 911, and four firemen stood around me as I was screaming and almost delirious. They tried to move me, but it was so painful, so they said they just couldn't help me but that an ambulance was on its way, and they would stay until it arrived. What a scene! I felt so bad for the kids, especially Jeremy and Joel who were only four and five years old, but I couldn't help it. The ambulance arrived, and on the way to the ER, I begged to have the woman stretch my arm out and I would relax as much as possible. Mark had been able to do it, why couldn't she?

Anyway, the woman in the ambulance said, "If we were in a field far away from the hospital, I would do it. But we are only several miles away, and I have to wait." But seeing the agony I was in, she whispered in my ear, "Don't tell anyone," and snap … my arm was back in, and I could think straight again! I thanked her over and over. When arriving at the hospital, they said if it hadn't gone back in when it did, because of the length of time it was out, my arm had become so swollen that it would have taken surgery to put it back in. Phew!

Many tears were shed, so many that I reached a point where I couldn't cry anymore. But the Lord was always faithful and in perfect timing to meet our needs. When it seemed like He wasn't there, He was reassuring us that He was always mindful! He saw us when I didn't think He did.

At some point, Mark took a standing position at a particular spot in the living room and stopped talking. He would walk to the bathroom and then come back to the same spot, hanging his head down. Sometimes he would sit silently for maybe five to ten minutes at the kitchen table when we were eating, but mostly he stood in that same spot all day long. This went on for three to four years. The first couple of years he would eat and then go back to the living room and stand. Eventually, he didn't even eat much on his own. I could tell he was hungry, so I tried to feed him. But he'd just smirk and let the food dribble down his face and laugh. So frustrating! I stopped doing that. We played in other rooms and lived life around his being this way.

When Jeremy was about four, he'd made a drawing. He was so proud of it, and ran up to Mark saying, "Daddy, look what I did!"

Mark just looked the other way. It broke my heart, and Jeremy was so confused. I tried to encourage Jeremy, saying how great his drawing was! I was so angry at Mark's response, and I hurt for Jeremy. These were the kind of moments that really caused me to try to protect the boys from Mark.

There were some rare times when Mark agreed to leave his standing spot on the living room floor to go to the grocery store with the boys and me. It was always a fiasco. We'd begin walking out to the car with the cart full of groceries, and Mark would suddenly stop in the middle of the parking lot with his head hung down. He refused to move! People around would stare at *me* like *I'm* the crazy one. Looking at me as if saying, "What is wrong with you, woman? Why are you even with him?" Like I'm supposed to know what to do? And the boys would try to coax him along to start walking. I couldn't leave him there. I couldn't get him walking, put the groceries in the car, *and* get the boys in their car seats all at once. But I had to do something. I decided to get the boys and groceries in the car first. Then I went back to rally him, escorting him by the arm to the car. Such an embarrassing time and so awkward. He seemed to know what he was doing, and that made me mad!

I finally made the decision to sell Mark's shop. It was clear that he would never be able to return to it, and selling it was the only source of money we had left. The buyer made monthly payments, and that gave me a predictable amount of money to budget with. We had no other means of financial help, including no government help, because we owned the home, and I didn't want to lose that. The monthly payments had to last as long as they could and barely covered our basic bills and essential foods. Then my washer broke down, and I had to buy a new one on credit. We had no extra, so I squeezed twenty-five dollars each month from the grocery budget to pay for the washer, not knowing how God would make up the difference.

One day things were so scary in the house I bundled the boys up and walked, pushing them in our double stroller, to Shadle Shopping Center, which was about a mile and a half away. It was so cold out. I felt so alone. So desperate. Where were we going to get money? I pleaded with God for help. I wished I could just go get a job, but Mark would freak out! What would I do? I couldn't call my parents or family. I was too embarrassed to ask my friends since they were helping so much all the time. But we needed money. One answer came that very week. A receipt from Sears came in the mail saying my balance on the washer was zero dollars! There had been over four hundred dollars remaining on the account. And it had been completely paid off! I found out much later that my good friend Wes had paid it off. 🙌🙌

There were several times when Mark was home that I witnessed some real demonic manifestations. Fear gripped him when he hallucinated, and it frequently caused him to snap to a seated position from sleep. Looking so frightened, he'd yell out, "I'm tormented by evil voices. They won't stop!" His eyes would twirl with a yellowish color. Despite this, I was determined to sleep in our bed with him. The boys had separate rooms when Joel was a baby, and then we put them together into one room. Anyway, I remember it being very tempting to just sleep in the spare room, but instead I prayed for God's protection and presence. I knew that "greater is He who is in you than he who is in the world," (1 John 4:4 NASB), and I was determined not to surrender to fear.

One night in particular, Mark sat up suddenly like he had had a nightmare. I asked him if he was all right and he turned and looked at me. For an instant, his eyes turned greenish and twirling. There was such an evil look in his expression. It was very frightening.… I began praying inside my mind and rehearsing, "Greater is He who is in me than he who is in the world." A tangible partition, like an invisible wall between us slid across the center of our bed. I'm telling you, it is as vivid to me now as it was then! Peace flooded my soul! I learned that intercession was critical! I continually prayed for protection over the boys and over myself.

Sometimes when I was singing as I did dishes and the boys were at the table behind me, Mark would come in from the spot he'd been standing in all day in the living room and he would be completely red in the face with his finger pressed up hard against his mouth, eyes bulging with rage, demonstrating that he insisted I be quiet! Many times it was when I was talking to the boys, urging them to eat. It was scary. They were still babies.… I had to talk!

When I married Mark, I was determined to never leave. I had made a vow to marry him, and I would keep it. Also, I grew up believing that divorce was wrong and not an option, so in all these difficulties, my mind never went there—until he wouldn't allow me to talk to the boys while feeding them. At this point, I had the first thought of divorce. I stayed hopeful he would change. And as I read the Bible at night, I'd be comforted by Scriptures such as Isaiah 41:10, which happens to be my favorite life verse, even now. It says, "Do not fear, for I am with you; do not be dismayed, for I am your God. I will strengthen you and help you; I will uphold you with my righteous right hand."

One time my good friend Cheri came walking through our living room, wearing a big smile, carrying many bags of groceries she purchased for us. Mark didn't seem thrilled or responsive at all. But I sure was! We were getting down to hardly any food, and I was running out of ideas. Cheri was such a blessing, coming unexpectedly at the perfect time. She commented that she was tempted to hang her coat on Mark standing there. It made me laugh. I needed a laugh right then, and I knew she understood my pain of this going on for years.

We had some other funny times that made me laugh. I always prayed and sang over the boys before they went to sleep. When Joel was two, he popped up to kiss me while I was leaning down to kiss him! Pain shot through my nose as I heard a big *crunch*. My nose was broken! Ouch! My doctor saw the X-ray and said, "There's nothing you can do for a broken nose but just wait it out." I had evidence of how much my little boy loved me every time I looked in the mirror. Black eyes and a crooked nose!

Another memorable time was when Jeremy was four and Joel was three. He put a Lego up Joel's nose! Fortunately, when I took Joel into the hospital emergency, the doctor was someone I went all through elementary and high school with, and he treated us with such care. He also lived down the street from us, which was another perk! He said he would have had to do a small surgery if it was a clear Lego, but fortunately, Jeremy picked the right color—a yellow one! He got it out just fine with a long tweezer with no further need for care. Success!

As the kids and I continued to live life around Mark's bizarre behavior, he would never shower, and his legs, which were already thin, became even thinner at the thighs and thicker and swollen at the calves. He developed multiple ulcers on his legs that would ooze poison. One particularly large ulcer developed on one of his swollen calves and produced a large amount of pus. The wounds began to fill our home with the stench of decaying flesh. I was growing very weak and went to my doctor. He said I really should leave Mark for the sake of my boys and myself. "If you don't, the boys won't have a daddy, which they don't have one as it stands, *or* a mommy."

CHAPTER THIRTEEN

The Joy of Knowing Christ

Mark's health was deteriorating, and I was reminded by the medical professionals that he had been born with a hole in his heart, which was still evident, and this was not something to mess around with, considering his lack of circulation and the ulcers on his legs. Then someone else at that time told me that I could be charged with murder if he died because I was *the responsible one.* I don't know if that person was a professional or not, but I was reminded over and over by mental health professionals that I was the responsible one, and since he was checked in as an involuntary patient, they held me accountable because he wouldn't get care on his own.

The last time I had to call mental health services, I instantly planned for the boys to be gone somewhere when they arrived to take Mark. When the mental health person came, they tried asking Mark questions first, which was always the pattern. But when he chose to not answer, they would refer all the questions to me. I had just sold the shop for as much money as I could get, since it had been sitting for over a year vacant and in extremely cold temperatures. I had to do something. We could not afford to wait another winter, plus we needed an income! I had not told Mark yet. I didn't think he'd respond or care anyway.

The mental health person had Mark sit down next to her and across from me. He kept his head and eyes turned down. This was normal. She asked me how I was, and I was honest.

"I can't do this anymore. I have to take care of our boys."

"Will you walk at least a mile a day with Mark to get his circulation going?"

"No, and he wouldn't go if I tried."

"Will you shower him or make sure that he is clean and the oozing ulcers are cleaned every day?"

"Ma'am, I can't. It's what he needs to do by showering. I don't have the strength and barely enough as it stands to take care of our two boys. And I can't force him."

The woman turned to Mark. "Will you commit to doing these things yourself? These ulcers are very dangerous to your health."

As usual, he had no response.

She continued to ask other questions.

No response.

Then she said, "Well then, we need you, Georgia, to go put some clothes together for him. We will have to take him to get him the care he needs. Do you have any income for you and the boys?"

"No, none at all. But I just sold the motorcycle shop Mark used to run."

Mark's head snapped up, his eyes blazing, and his face flushing a deep red. "You what?"

That was the first time I had heard his voice in months, maybe years. Yep, a very clear response came from him then.

I got up and proceeded to go into our room and get his clothes together. He immediately got up and followed me and cornered me against the wall and tried with all his might to strangle me ... but his hands were unable to touch my throat. I had such a peace that flowed through me! I did not say a word but knew I was safe. The Lord was so present there, and all I could do was smile at Mark. In my mind the words kept repeating with great assurance, *You can't harm me.… Greater is He that is in me than he that is in the world.* I'll never forget that real, tangible presence of God within me. Such a peace flooded me. His power was so evident because I knew the puzzling look on Mark's face was evidence that he had nothing in him that was trying to *stop* the strangling. Everything in him wanted to choke me. He was so confused when his hands could not touch my throat, as much as he wanted them to. Once again, there was a divine wall of protection.

During the seven years I lived with Mark, there were times I felt so trapped, like in a prison. I prayed once that the Lord would just take Mark. Actually, I found myself praying that often at one point. I was so sick of all of this. Then I felt bad that I was praying for him to die … and yet what was really happening was that I was dying, learning to rely solely on God to fill every part of me. God became closer to me than ever before, just like He promised during the original vision of the narrow path; nothing beyond but Mark, and I would suffer if I chose this way, but the joy I'd have in knowing Christ would be greater than any other way would bring.

It always hurt to see Mark taken away because it was hard on him, but there were no other options. Deep down, he was a sweet man, and he loved God, but there were also so many tragic times in his past that paralyzed him.

After that last time he was taken away, I had an opportunity to learn more from his dad, Ben, because we both had to go to several court hearings out at Eastern State Hospital to testify about him so they could appoint a legal guardian. He confirmed everything Mark had told me about his past, with his first wife, Helen, dying of leukemia and his second wife, Helen, committing suicide. He added that she also had been in and out of the psychiatric hospital after they divorced.

When Mark was admitted to the psychiatric hospital the final time, I called my dad immediately. I realized that now I *could* call him without any hassle from Mark. I was free—at least to do this! He was teaching an architecture drafting course at Gonzaga University. This was a day to remember! I asked if I could come meet him, and he said, "Of course, Georgie! Come meet me for lunch!" I had not been in touch with Dad for at least six years and had been unable to have any kind of a relationship with him or Mom because of Mark. He was thrilled and so was I! He and my mom had continued saying many prayers for us. They had also had their hearts shattered by this whole situation, especially not being able to be a part of our lives.

When I met up with Dad, the first thing I said, as I broke, was how sorry I was that he and Mom had to go through so much pain. I knew my marriage to Mark broke their hearts. He was right that he saw something not right about him, and he had tried to warn me. I did reiterate to him that I still believed God wanted me to marry Mark, as hard as it might be to believe that. Plus, I couldn't imagine life without Jeremy and Joel. He said he forgave me for sure and that as soon as we could, we should visit his friend who was a lawyer.

We went either the next day or later that day and the lawyer started trying to convince me to not just legally separate but to divorce. I had a real problem with that suggestion, but he pointed out why and eventually convinced me that separation was no protection for me or the boys, and that divorce would protect me from getting all of Mark's medical bills or hassle from him the rest of his life. Even though we were married outside the Catholic church, that wasn't enough for my heart to be at peace. I knew I could not live with him anymore, so this divorce would be a way to be final. I agreed to go for the divorce.

Through time, I began seeing and accepting things more clearly. Someone suggested I talk with an older woman whom I did not know well but who was very knowledgeable of the Bible. As I explained how I didn't feel right about divorce, she pointed me to a Scripture that really set me free—Numbers 30:3–5. It says,

> When a young woman still living in her father's household makes a vow to the LORD or obligates herself by a pledge and her father hears about her vow or pledge but says nothing to her, then all her vows and every pledge by which she obligated herself will stand. *But if her father forbids her when he hears about it, none of her vows or the pledges by which she obligated herself will stand; the LORD will release her because her father has forbidden her.*

She also talked and prayed with me, and I knew in my heart that there was a peace about the divorce and felt the leading of the Holy Spirit, and I now had confirmation from the Word of God. I had never wanted to marry anyone without my dad's blessing. Plus, I knew that for the boys' sake and my health, I needed to leave him for good.

Before a legal guardian had been appointed, I was still considered the responsible person for him. While the divorce was pending, I received a call from an apartment manager where Mark was put in after the hospital released him, since I was no longer picking him up. The manager told me Mark was scaring people because he was roaming around completely nude. Police were called, but they saw his past background and came to put him back in the apartment. Things would be fine with him not coming out for a while, but that didn't last. So at one point that winter, they asked me to come and see if I could reason with him. Of course, I knew that I couldn't, but I would try, just once. I arrived late on that frosty day, and no lights were on. I thought maybe he was gone. But I knocked anyway, and there he was, standing somewhat aloof in the dark, with just a pair of shorts on. And it was so cold in the apartment!

"Mark! Why haven't you turned on the heat?"

He looked at me quizzically. "I hadn't thought of that."

"What about the lights? It's dark as night in here."

"I don't need light."

I shook my head. "Look, I know you've been walking around outside nude. Your apartment manager called me and said you're going to be kicked out if he gets any more reports from your neighbors. He's not giving you any more warnings. This is it, Mark. You've got to stop going outside naked. Just close your curtains, keep your clothes on, and stay inside."

I believe shortly after that encounter, he was hospitalized again until a legal guardian was appointed by the courts.

It took one and a half years of court hearings before the divorce could be final. There had to be a lawyer appointed by the judge who would be willing to be Mark's guardian. He would be paid for his part by the state. It took seven lawyers before one agreed and became his guardian. He looked after Mark's well-being, getting him housing and meeting his financial and medical needs.

During this time of waiting for finality, the boys and I continued to live in the same house, and I surrounded myself with friends. Even more importantly, I could actually see my family again! My parents; my two youngest siblings, *the babies*, Frank (twenty-two) and Cathy (twenty-one); and Jeremy, Joel, and I drove a motor home my dad rented from a friend to Disneyland, including Ghirardelli Square, one of our favorite stops on the way back. It was such a fun and memorable trip!

CHAPTER FOURTEEN

Her Mother and I

There were many people from our church who cared about us like family. Wes was one of them and became my close friend, like a brother. One day, however, Wes was sitting on a chair in my kitchen talking with one of the boys. As they ran off after showing him the Lego car they made, he quickly pulled me down on his lap.

Whoa! 😳 I had totally forgotten what a man felt like! I'll never forget my reaction.… As I gently scratched his arm, I said, "You're so hairy; I love it!" But being held like that, *wowza*. I melted, but I also knew I had to be very careful.

I quickly stood up. The divorce had not been finalized; I was still married, and he was a single guy. His clear blue eyes held so much love for me, and it scared me. Oh, how I loved every second of it, but this couldn't happen. "Wes, I don't want to lead you on. I don't think I can ever remarry. You have so much going for you, and I am such a mess. I know you really care about us but …" I didn't really want to say these words, but I didn't want to hurt his heart by leading him on. So, I said it. "I can never look to you as a husband."

Well, that didn't stick, and I'm glad, because he's the best thing that's ever happened to me. This broken mess had pure love coming toward me, someone genuinely in love with me. And my boys! That meant *so* much!

My heart began to heal and have hope again. Recently, I found this picture from around that time that I gave to Wes with a message on back.

Joel 3 years old, Jeremy 4.5 years old (1986)

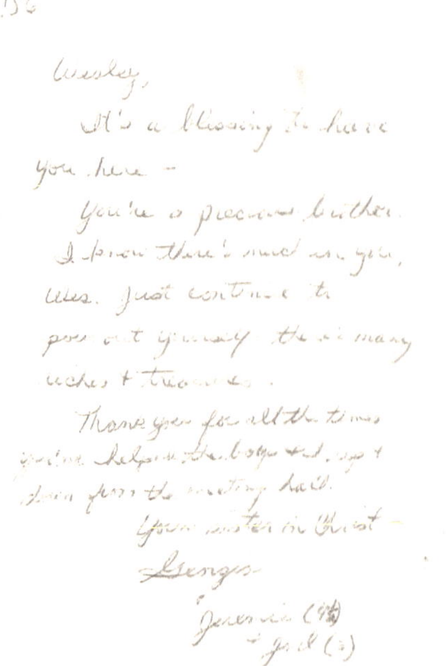

Message I wrote on the back of the photo to Wes

My divorce from Mark was eventually finalized, and one month before I turned thirty-one, I happily married Wesley Howard Morris on May 5, 1990! 👏👏 I'll always remember my dad's voice rehearsing as we walked arm and arm down the aisle in the church. "Her mother and I, her mother and I." He made me giggle, and what joy flooded my heart to know he was given the opportunity to give me away properly to the man he felt right about. I now had his and my mom's total blessing! And their broken hearts were mended.

Dad walking me down the aisle

Our wedding candle says, "On this day, I will marry my friend, the one I laugh with, live for, and love." He truly has been my best friend, seeing, accepting, and loving me when I was at my lowest place and bringing such life and joy.

Jeremy and Joel were so thrilled, and they participated in our wedding, carrying our pillows with rings attached. Jeremy had just turned eight, and Joel was almost seven. Jeremy even drew us as a bride and groom with hearts all around us, and he wrote, "Thay will stay happy!!"

Jeremy's drawing, age eight

We still keep that on our wall in our bedroom. It's pretty special! After we were married, both boys asked if they could call Uncle Wes "Daddy" now. It really warmed my heart, and I said of course! They started calling Mark "Daddy Mark" after Wes and I got married. Wes was Daddy!

Our new family

Our wedding party—Bridesmaids: Mary Kay (sister), Cheri (best friend), Susie (sister); Flower girls: Bekah and Rachel (my nieces, Susie's daughters); Men: Wally, Scott (Wes's brothers), and Frank (my brother); Ring bearers: Joel and Jeremy

We went to Maui for our honeymoon, and it was such a fun time! It's a cute story Wes likes to tell. He won a two-week stay from his work over a year before our wedding. That particular day, I had decided to take the boys to see Uncle Wes's workplace. It was five o'clock, and one of his coworkers pointed us to the closed door where Wes and the others were meeting. From the hallway, we heard, "And the winner is … Wes Morris," and everyone cheered! Then they all came out, and Wes saw us standing there. This was our first visit there. He had the biggest smile from ear to ear!

He said, "I just won a trip to Maui for two people!"

Of course, things were still on hold for my divorce to be final. I responded, "Oh, that's great! That'll be so fun. I wonder who you'll go with?"

Later on, when people asked him, "Who are you going to take?" he'd say, "Well, been thinking of taking Georgia's brother Frank."

"*Ha!* You better not!" I'd reply once we were engaged.

My friend Cheri, the one who brought all the groceries, was my maid of honor, and my two oldest sisters, Mary Kay and Susie, were my bridesmaids. My brother Jim and our friend Karl both played guitar and sang with my little sister, Cathy. My sister Linda's son had his first birthday that same day. We had a little cake for him at the reception as well. The church was filled with lots of close friends and relatives.

Cheri was gracious to pick up our wedding clothes from the airport hotel where we spent our first night … and Wes carried me over the threshold!

Then off we flew! We had fun in the sun. We spent two weeks in Maui, and I got to be the one to go (*not my brother, ha!*). We even tried parasailing, and I snorkeled while Wes went scuba diving. We loved every minute!

Honeymoon in Maui

Early into our marriage, Mark's guardian asked Wes if he wanted to be appointed as the visitation guardian. On the visiting Saturdays, Mark might play with the boys for the first hour, and then Wes would take over for the next two hours when Mark just stopped or for the remainder of the time. After about a year of seeing Mark every other Saturday for several hours, the boys asked if they could not see him anymore. They really wanted to play only with Daddy (Wes).

Anyway, it was a difficult situation for sure, but I asked the lawyer about it, and he said that the boys did not have to continue seeing him as long as *they* voiced that to Mark. They were then only eight and nine years old. Each of them did tell him in their own way, and I'll never forget when they came back with Wes. They all described how they got to run up the Suncrest Hill (nicknamed Big Sandy), and they were flooded with joy!

Joy was brought to my heart and into all our hearts with Kenny being born! He had and still has the greatest smile. Loved his little chuckle when tickling him. I was also very happy that my parents could be at the hospital and freely be involved in our lives.

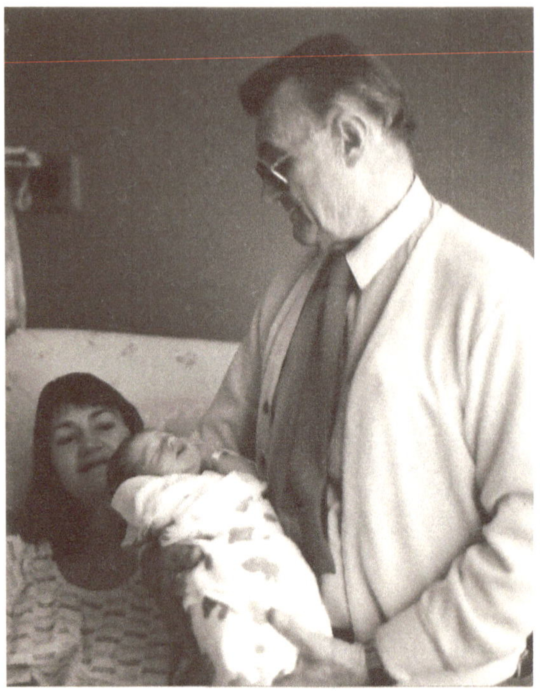

My dad (Grandpa Swoboda) holding baby Kenny

*Jeremy pushing Joel and Kenny in a go-cart made by Grandpa Ben,
Suncrest home, 1993*

I was pregnant again when Kenny was one, but Wes and I lost our second baby at four months along. I couldn't grieve. It was painfully hard, but I felt numb. I kept myself busy loving the other three boys. One day when I was alone in the car, I asked God to help me. I felt bad that I couldn't cry or feel anything. Just numb. Then a special song came on the Christian radio station. I had never heard it before, and though I and others have searched for it since, I have never heard it again. The words had a message, saying something like, "Thank you for giving me life, Mama, because now I am in heaven, and I'm with Jesus." Its lyrics just touched my heart and broke open the dam. I was able to release all my sadness with tears, and many of them. I even called the station and asked what it was called and gave them the time I heard it. When I had done this before, they could always look at their list and tell me the song, but not this time. I received it as a gift from heaven.

Three months later, I was pregnant with Katie. Such joy once again. I had the girl I told my mom about many years before.☺ "Katie" Rose—*Katherine,* meaning pure, and *Rose,* the symbol of love. Pure Love, and she sure is. My Grandma Swoboda's name was Catherine (she went by Katie, with a *K*!), and I was pregnant with Katie when she was starting to fail physically, but she was a sharp lady until the end! She spent time at our home after Grandpa had died, and I also had lived with her in her home when I was in college before living with the girls in my other grandma's house. Wes even lived with her for a short time when we were engaged. She meant so much to us, and I told her that if I had a baby girl, I was going to name her Katie, after her. She passed a few months before Katie was born.

When Katie was born, I was ecstatic to hear, "It's a girl!" Wes's dad always told me we'd never have a girl because there were only boys on his side of the family. I proved him wrong, ha ha! We all were excited, including Grandpa Wally.☺ The first thought that came to my mind when they brought her to me was, *she has a keen mind.* That was an odd thing to think, since I rarely used the word *keen*, if ever. She's that way though, very bright.

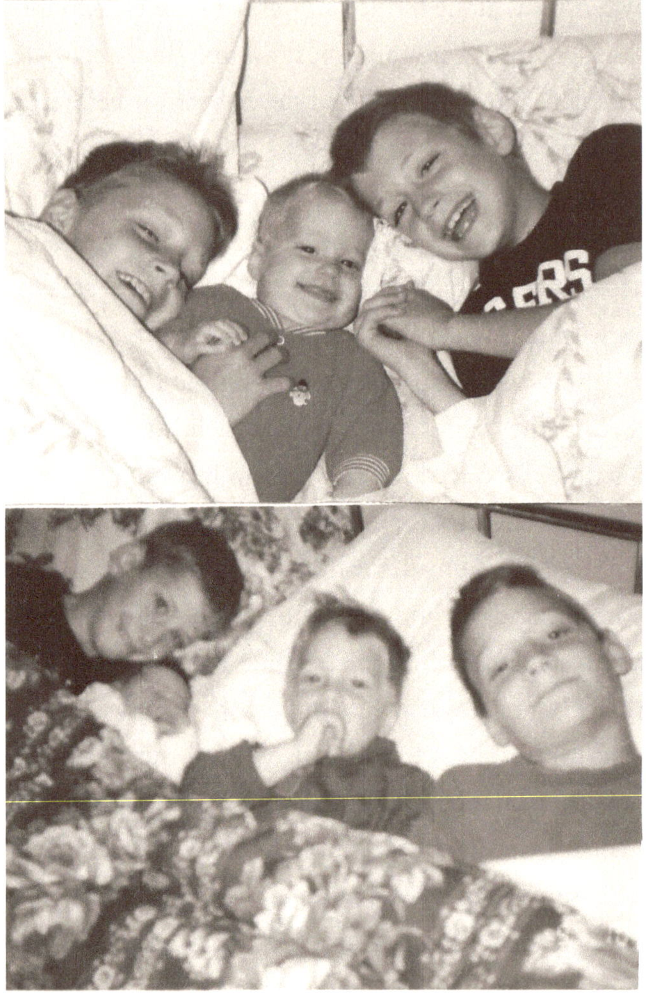

Three boys (baby Kenny), three boys and baby Katie

We traveled with all four kids to St. Louis, Missouri, once a year or so to visit Wes's family. He grew up about fifteen miles from St. Louis in a village across the river on the Illinois side called Millstadt. Wes has two brothers, and his mother, Lois (who goes by Pat), is still living. Both of our dads passed away a month apart in 2008. It was always fun to hear the kids laugh at Grandpa Wally's jokes. We sure miss him. And my mom, Lois, passed in 2018. We always thought it special that our moms were both named Lois.

Wes traveled a lot for his job. Sometimes it was difficult for me raising two toddlers and two middle schoolers with him gone a lot. But we worked through it and did the best we could. I finished my last few classes for my bachelor of arts degree in music (K–12), adding classes to get endorsements as a K–12 reading specialist and in K–8 classroom education. This all occurred while Kenny and Katie were toddlers. I was home most days, but a couple of days per week, I had to travel to the university and leave the kids with a trusted daycare. It was a busy time but helped in healing the old scars of not being able to finish school.

There was a preschool that met in the basement of our church that had been established for several years, and they asked if I would be interested in starting a kindergarten. I agreed! I taught Kenny's class of twelve students while Katie was in the preschool. That was my first job after getting my credentials. Later, I got a job teaching music at a Christian elementary school. Kenny and Katie went there as well. And then I taught in public schools for many years after that as a music specialist. It was fun to be able to work in the schools with my own kiddos also there.

Our four kids played soccer, and the boys played baseball and basketball. Katie had dance and gymnastics along with soccer. We were involved with church and had small group in our home as well as enjoying the company of neighbors, friends, and family. And on Easter, we would have Easter egg hunts in our backyard and then play a big baseball game at the elementary school across the street with our large extended family. I taught music at Northwest Christian, and we eventually invited the principal's family to join our baseball game. We discovered when I was hired that we lived only two blocks away from each other, and we became close friends with them, and we still are! In fact, their daughter Jenell is now Jeremy's wife! We love Jenell and were thrilled when Jeremy proposed. We even traveled to England with her parents before Jenell and Jeremy got married, and since then, we've all gone to Africa together as well. And one of the best parts is … we share three amazing grandchildren!

We are also very close to the family of Kimberlee, who is now Joel's wife. They met when they were freshmen in high school. They were both passionate about getting students together at the large public school they attended to learn about God. It started around the flagpole with prayer and then graduated to meeting in a classroom before school, studying the Bible, and then on Friday nights to full services in the auditorium! Wes and I met our now daughter-in-law Kimberlee's parents at one of those Friday night services. We discovered we lived very close to each other. They came to our small group in our home, and we grew together as friends as well as with Jenell's parents. And then Joel and Kimberlee went to the same Bible college in Minneapolis. They were married at nineteen and continued going to school for the next three years, living in the married apartments. Another fun fact … they share the same birthday and year!

Another fun thing we did as a family was to make rockets. Well, the kids would make rockets with Wes's help while I made cookies. ☺ And then we would send the rockets off in the schoolyard across the street. Neighbors would come over as well and help out, trying to catch them as they parachuted down. Then everyone came inside for cookies and hot chocolate!

There were times when life became difficult because of the pressures of work and children. But God was our lifeline. During some of these significant times, Wes and I had no words after many words, if you know what I mean. So we would hold hands and pray, even if we didn't want to. However, usually there was some time before we got around to doing that. But each time, God would move us forward, restoring peace with forgiveness, helping us communicate better, restoring happiness, helping us love each other better, and helping us understand each other. Life is not easy when juggling so much, but God can bring peace and wants to help. Taking the time to be together and pray was one of our anchors to keep us together, strong as a couple, strong as a family. It still is.

We also took time to read Scriptures as a family. When my dad was still living, he even asked Wes to lead the family Bible study! Dad was a committed Catholic, and Wes was raised Protestant, but that's how much my dad trusted Wes, even spiritually. And music and worship were a big part of our time together with the kids as they grew up.

Of course, we loved the parties and family times. Our family hosted Thanksgiving, Christmas, and Easter, sometimes including extra family or friends who had nowhere else to go. We threw baby showers, wedding showers, birthday parties.… We loved people and still do! We love playing outside, working puzzles, and playing games—from card games to board games and other strategy games that Wes likes to play with the boys and grandsons too!

Remember those long wooden skis that my dad got us kids? Now our kids had snowboards—all three boys. And I had skis and also drove them up to the mountain until they got their licenses. My skis were a lot shorter though, ha ha!

Wes and I served together on a worship team, as youth leaders, and as small group leaders. We took long walks, had long talks, and cheered our children on at their sporting events. He even helped coach soccer. While raising our kids and working, I got my master's in education, and Wes got his MBA and also his pilot's license. We flew to see Joel's family in Lakeview, Oregon, from eastern Washington! We also took rides over Idaho, seeing beautiful lakes and mountains there. Over the years, we had fun! And we still do, especially traveling to many different countries. Although we did eventually sell our part of the Cessna, we still fly on the big airplanes.

Jeremy, as a teenager, was always building things. I'm sure the Legos helped in his earlier years. He is highly creative and built a cage that kept getting bigger and bigger for his iguana. Eventually, he moved his bed into the closet under the stairs because the plexiglass cage was so large. The iguana grew to about three feet long. Little did any of us know Jeremy would eventually live in Africa where they roam freely! He and Joel enjoyed riding bikes and building forts. All the kids loved sledding in the winter and swimming in the summer. There were typical trials with all four kids—some were very intense—but we always grew closer through them with each other.

After we'd been married eleven years, Wes and I went to the Czech Republic to visit our former pastor, who had married us, and his wife. They were serving in an international church for five years in Budapest. My great-grandpa and great-grandma Svoboda were from villages in the Czech Republic, about forty miles from Prague. Great-Grandpa was from Strážnice, and Great-Grandma from Hodonín. One of the cities still has a wall around it. The entrances to the villages they lived in were only about a block away from each other. We all took a drive to see the area where they had lived, and we got to meet some distant relatives who were still living in Strážnice. We visited for three hours, with the help of their granddaughter who came over to interpret. We shared pictures of my dad who looked so much like the man in front of us. We could see the oppression from the war still on their faces and saw how much hardship they still dealt with in the village. It was no longer Czechoslovakia but now renamed Czech Republic. It made me appreciate my "liberty" heritage even more.

When the boys became adults (nineteen and twenty), during Father's Day week, without talking to each other, they both legally changed their last name to Morris, taking on Wes's last name. Joel was living in Minneapolis in college, and Jeremy was in Spokane. We went to Minneapolis to visit Joel, and he surprised us with a court setting. It was really cute, because the judge asked Katie and Kenny, ages eight and eleven, if they would agree to receive Joel as their big brother (even though they had already thought he was their full brother). It was such an amazing time! We found out after getting back to Spokane that Jeremy had changed his name too! Wes has truly been a gem to all of us.

Morris family, 2002

CHAPTER FIFTEEN

What I Wish I Had Known

While I was writing this book, I decided to look into what is medically known about schizophrenia. I had never done this before because I just tried to survive it caring for Mark. I recently found a book that resonated with me called *Surviving Schizophrenia*, by E. Fuller Torrey, MD,[1] on Audible and listened over the course of four months. The book triggered many of the memories I've recorded here, dredging up the deep pain and torment I went through, but it made so many of the things Mark did make more sense.

Over and over, Dr. Torrey reiterated that there was no research, and efforts were not made toward helping patients with this disease during the 1980s, the period when I lived with Mark. No wonder his hospital visits were a revolving door with no follow-up. Since then, there have

---

1. E. Fuller Torrey, *Surviving Schizophrenia: A Family Manual*, 6th ed. (New York: Harper Perennial, 2013), Audible audio ed., read by Matthew Josdal (Old Saybrook, CT: Tantor Audio, 2018). All subsequent citations refer to this edition.

been more support groups and advocates in and out of the medical field, especially in the 1990s. But we still have a big problem in our society of not valuing people with schizophrenia. In the last chapter of the book, Dr. Torrey makes it clear that unless something is done, people with schizophrenia will continue as fourth-class citizens, often shunned and neglected.[2]

In general, people don't understand instances like when Mark would bizarrely stop in the parking lot of the grocery store. I felt so isolated and alone. Dr. Torrey writes about how important it is for caregivers, family, or friends of someone with schizophrenia to have support, or they can become completely drained.[3] No joke! I know I would have loved to have had the support of other people experiencing what I was going through. There may have been some out there, but I never knew of any and surely wasn't given resources to help connect me. I was so confused by what was happening with Mark, and it was never explained to me that his brain was breaking down. I'm thankful to see there are more resources and support groups now.[4]

Learning, even so long after my marriage to him, that Mark's behavior was typical for people with his disease gave me a deep sense of comfort. It helps me even now, as I look back, to have confirmation that this is a physical sickness in addition to a spiritual issue, and Mark's progression from bad to worse is exactly what medical professionals now expect to see when a patient is not treated.[5] It's actually now known that a diagnosis of manic depression, which was Mark's original diagnosis, can change to schizophrenia if the disease is prolonged.[6]

---

2.   Torrey, *Surviving Schizophrenia*, 14 hr. 58 min.

3.   Torrey, *Surviving Schizophrenia*, 14 hr. 57 min.

4.   Torrey, *Surviving Schizophrenia*, 15 hr. 30 min.; 15 hr. 24 min.; 10 hr. 56 min.

5.   Torrey, *Surviving Schizophrenia*, 15 hr. 19 min.; 13 hr. 50 min.

6.   Torrey, *Surviving Schizophrenia*, 13 hr. 54 min.

The human mind needs a filter for a person to function properly in this world. But with those who suffer from schizophrenia, there is a breakdown in the filter.[7] Their mind is highly sensitive, hearing every noise, and there is over-acuteness of all of their senses.[8] Their hearing and vision are all impaired. And touch makes some of them feel like they are being electrocuted.[9] Their senses feel constantly overwhelmed. This certainly explains Mark's angry shushing of me at mealtimes when I'd try to talk to the boys.

Schizophrenia also causes them to be bombarded with intrusive thoughts. They even go so far as to believe other people are inserting thoughts into their heads.[10] They experience a paranoia that they're always being watched.[11] And it feels very real to them that those around them are against them and critical of them, no matter how nice, kind, and supportive those people are.[12] It makes it hard to socialize. A person may cough in the room, and the person with schizophrenia may take it personally, triggering suspicious delusions. And unfortunately, it is usually not possible to reason with delusional people.[13] These symptoms may be what caused Mark to force me to cut ties with my family and eventually his parents as well.

The neural changes in their brains also cause depression and guilt. They become withdrawn and isolated. Fear is pervasive. And uncontrollable, exaggerated feelings bombard them. They have no ability to express these intense emotions. It's just too hard to communicate. It's easier if they

---

7. Torrey, *Surviving Schizophrenia*, 13 hr. 53 min.; 13 hr. 24 min.
8. Torrey, *Surviving Schizophrenia*, 15 hr. 13 min.; 13 hr. 52min.
9. Torrey, *Surviving Schizophrenia*, 15 hr. 10 min.
10. Torrey, *Surviving Schizophrenia*, 13 hr. 50 min.
11. Torrey, *Surviving Schizophrenia*, 15 hr. 22 min; 13 hr. 51 min.
12. Torrey, *Surviving Schizophrenia*, 15 hr. 23 min.
13. Torrey, *Surviving Schizophrenia*, 13 hr. 49 min.

just stay still. Their thoughts get jumbled up, so why try? Being still is easier. This initiates a catatonic state, immobilizing them in one place.[14] This is what happened to Mark for at least three or more years. Their lack of communication and silence can make it seem they are completely out of touch, but they can really hear everything. What could be more frustrating to a loving family than this?[15]

On the other end of the spectrum, flattened emotions prevent them from empathizing with those around them. They are unable to put themselves in other people's shoes, are unaware of anyone else's feelings, and can be very stubborn.[16] This helped explain Mark's rejection of my lovingly crafted and carefully created Mod Podge present. Also, when he turned his head away from looking at Jeremy's drawing when he tried to show him. And the many voices they are processing in their minds sometimes prompt them to laugh at highly inappropriate times.[17]

Disrobing in front of others can also be a response to voices threatening them that if they don't do this, as well as other bizarre acts, the world will end or that they need to do these acts to fight against materialism or some kind of threat that convinces them they must obey these impulses.[18] Experts and loved ones who are not familiar with schizophrenia can easily believe these tormented souls feel nothing at all. In reality, they are overwhelmed. There are too many feelings, so in many ways they just shut down.[19]

In addition to emotional shutdown, the pain receptors in their brain become blocked by the disease. Many patients deliberately do not

---

14. Torrey, *Surviving Schizophrenia*, 15 hr. 20 min.; 13 hr. 56 min.

15. Torrey, *Surviving Schizophrenia*, 10 hr. 54 min.

16. Torrey, *Surviving Schizophrenia*, 13 hr. 50 min.

17. Torrey, *Surviving Schizophrenia*, 13 hr. 49 min.; 11 hr. 40 min.

18. Torrey, *Surviving Schizophrenia*, 12 hr. 23 min.

19. Torrey, *Surviving Schizophrenia*, 11 hr. 34 min.

shower or clean themselves for weeks, as was the case with Mark.[20] Their lack of movement or exercise can cause perforated ulcers to develop, and their refusal to stay clean can contribute to infection, but because their pain receptors are blocked, it is common for them to feel no pain at all.[21]

There is so much misery and suffering, and it's easy to blame the sick person for causing the hurt. Some families aren't aware that this is a disease with a biological component, that people don't cause schizophrenia. It's a chronic disease of the brain. But in families who are aware of this, healthy members may struggle with shame for being angry at the family member who is in such suffering. Although experiencing blame may be unavoidable, blaming each other or ourselves is harmful, not helpful. Right attitudes help families survive.[22] And showing grace and patience, to ourselves first and then to others, will go a long way in fueling endurance. Advice like this would have really helped me through those years.

It's clear to see that all members of the family suffer when one family member has schizophrenia.[23] One of the members has been healthy and productive and then gradually or suddenly changes. The family keeps hoping and waiting and wondering when they will return to normalcy. But they get worse.[24] It can cause anger at God for creating a world that has this illness in it. Bitterness can turn inward and cause depression.[25] If the husband is the affected member, the wife becomes his guardian and the head of the household, which comes with its own

20. Torrey, *Surviving Schizophrenia*, 11 hr. 48 min.
21. Torrey, *Surviving Schizophrenia*, 13 hr. 52 min.; 13 hr. 38 min.
22. Torrey, *Surviving Schizophrenia*, 15 hr. 20 min.; 10 hr. 56 min.
23. Torrey, *Surviving Schizophrenia*, 10 hr. 54 min.
24. Torrey, *Surviving Schizophrenia*, 11 hr. 14 min.
25. Torrey, *Surviving Schizophrenia*, 10 hr. 54 min.

set of considerations and stressors.[26] Healthy family members experience shame and embarrassment, especially if they don't understand what is happening. And even if they don't recognize it, they enter a perpetual state of mourning for a loved one who is still alive as if that loved one were dead. It is extraordinarily painful for everyone but can additionally create personal fear for children in the home, who may wonder if the sickness is genetic and if they will develop it.[27]

Dr. Torrey advises families who want to stay together that perspective matters: accepting things as they are and not as you wish they could be goes a long way in sustaining the family unit.[28] This helps families to weigh the needs of the person with schizophrenia and provide help for them, even though it is draining and stressful for those helping them.[29] Lowering expectations and embracing the idea that they'll never get better can help create less stress, but it creates a particular sadness too. Similar to how a family with a member who has polio can benefit from realizing that person will never walk normally again, accepting the member with schizophrenia as they are can eliminate undue energy from being channeled into exasperating efforts. Focusing on small joys and being grateful the family member with schizophrenia is alive rather than focusing on their weaknesses can help. Positive attitudes create an environment in which it is easier to feel love for them.

Dr. Torrey asserts, and I agree with him, that support groups help. I can't testify to this personally, though, because of the total lack of an awareness of support groups at the time I went through this. But now, organizations such as NAMI (National Alliance on Mental Illness)

---

26. Torrey, *Surviving Schizophrenia*, 11 hr. 30 min.
27. Torrey, *Surviving Schizophrenia*, 12 hr. 02 min.; 11hr. 58 min.
28. Torrey, *Surviving Schizophrenia*, 11 hr. 08 min.
29. Torrey, *Surviving Schizophrenia*, 11 hr. 09 min.

provide connections for family-to-family support.[30] From 1985 to the present, the number of support groups has grown tremendously. And support groups seem to be the main advocates for this illness—people who have lived with it or been a family member of one who suffers from it. The growing number of support groups work toward meeting the need to speak out and continue to care about patients and families affected by schizophrenia.

While I don't regret in any way how my story turned out, perhaps your story can go in a new, positive direction by learning all of this medical information that wasn't available to me then. There's so much more information included in Dr. Torrey's book than what I've referred to here, but these are the main points that resonated with my story.

---

30. Torrey, *Surviving Schizophrenia*, 11hr. 19 min.

CHAPTER SIXTEEN

My Final Thoughts

Dear reader,

I know as you read this, you may be feeling like what you're going through is so much worse than what I experienced and can never be changed. Please find hope. Please open up to the possibility of complete freedom. It may not happen in an instant, but my hope for you is that the chains of depression and hopelessness will be broken and that you will find true hope. We can't do this alone, but God is able to set us free completely inside, whether it be from pain from others or pain brought on by ourselves. We are living in a fallen world, but that doesn't mean we have to live downcast and full of fear. If we have the Spirit of God living in us, He is our light in the darkness. We are overcomers of evil, the head and not the tail. You are valued by God…. He sees you, created you, and knows more about you than any person ever can. Ask Him to help you and free you. He will.

In addition to uncovering memories through reading *Surviving Schizophrenia* by E. Fuller Torrey throughout the process of writing this book, I also sought counseling with Wes at my side. As triggers of past hurts surfaced, I had to identify with the help of counseling where these were coming from. Was it my current husband, Wes, or something lingering from my past that I might have projected onto Wes? Forgiveness is a key to healing after shedding light on relational problems, and sometimes we need advice from a third party, an objective view and professional guidance. Wes and I aren't perfect, but this process has brought us greater closeness with and understanding of each other. I also have been able to completely forgive Mark, but it hasn't happened all at once. I've gone through stages, and every time something comes up, I have to ask God to help me forgive him and then release him, the hurt, the memory. This goes for anyone who causes us pain. We are not free if we hold on to grudges or are critical of others. I've learned to have eyes to see others as if they are whole. That's the love and grace that God gives me. I'm not perfect and yet He still loves me. He is enough. I don't have to perform my way to be accepted or loved more.

So instead of a poem put on the altar, now my book is an offering in faith that God will multiply His sweet freedom to all who read this, no matter what you're going through. Matthew 19:26 says, "Jesus looked at them and said, 'With man this is impossible, but with God all things are possible.'" I love how it says Jesus *looked* at them. He sees you, my friend. He's personal and cares. And *all* things are possible with God, not just some.

I've lived through suffering. It doesn't mean that I am perfect now or don't have hard days, but that constant pressure of living under a dark cloud and the real presence of evil is gone. And that can be for any of us. I'm not unique. I'm a person just like you. At times I've cried deeply as I've written these pages, knowing that there are so many of you going through worse situations than I ever went through, but suffering is suffering. God knows, and He's able to reach down and rescue. I am confident of that for you. I am confident you will find your security in Him.

A Light from on high will dawn upon us.… To shine upon and give light to those who sit in darkness and in the shadow of death, to direct and guide our feet … into the way of peace. (Luke 1:78–79 AMPC)

Believe for your breakthrough!

Epilogue

Wes and I have been married almost thirty-four years now and have been blessed with four adult children, two amazing daughters-in-law, a wonderful son-in-law, and seven precious grandchildren. There came a day when we all spread out. No one lives in our area now (Seattle). We go to them, and at times they come to us. We soak in as much as we can because we understand they have busy lives as well. I love FaceTime … at least we have that for the in-between times until we can be in person.

Jeremy, Jenell, Paul (13), Wesley (11), Ellie (7)

Jeremy's building skills became great preparation for what he didn't see coming … a contractor career and eventually living in Africa for ten years and making such a difference for people there, using his building ability in ministry. Jenell has been faithfully homeschooling our three middle grandchildren, Paul, Wesley, and Ellie.

Joel married his high school sweetheart, Kimberlee, who shared his passion for prayer around the flagpole—they both worked together to lead many hundreds of high schoolers in prayer and Bible study. Now they have been married twenty years, still serving in ministry together. They are also very talented musicians. Their children are our two oldest grandsons, John and Andy, and are involved with music and technology and using their skills for God. Kimberlee has also been a very dedicated homeschool teacher all the boys' lives.

Joel and Kimberlee

Andy (15) and Johnny (17)

Kenny became an Eagle Scout (which takes a huge commitment) and has a very quick mind! He's quite witty, and it's no surprise he loves music as well. He started playing guitar at a young age, even as part of the worship team we had at Northwest Christian and then at his youth group. He also took some violin lessons!

Reading is a huge passion of his. He, along with Wes and his Uncle Wally, share a bi-weekly study of history. He also works out regularly, loves to run, and plays racquetball. Kenny works for a restaurant and loves to make people happy. We love staying with him and eating at the restaurant when we visit Spokane. At times, we've seen old friends there, and they always comment how they *love* Kenny and that he's the reason they eat there. I told you … he's got that winning smile, big heart, and is so great with people!

Kenny's thirtieth birthday picture

Katie was a long-distance runner in her high school, and she and her teammates were also state champions. She continues running, at times even pushing her four-and six-year old in a stroller as she runs. What a mom! She just turned thirty, and for her birthday she ran a 50K on the Oregon coast, starting along the beach for ten miles and then up into rugged trails in the forest, reaching the highest lookout on the Oregon coast—so hard, but she did it and came in fifth for women! We were able to witness it and cheer her on. She also teaches more than twenty-five piano students and is married to our son-in-law, Jordan, who is also a very talented musician, runner, coach, and businessman. I was thrilled when Katie asked me if she could wear my wedding dress. She made a couple of minor changes to the sleeves, and I *loved* what she did to make it her own and how beautiful she looked! The wedding was a beautiful time together. And we love Jordan and his family! It was such a blessing when Jeremy and his family traveled back from Africa to be with all of us for the wedding.

Left to right: Kimberlee, Joel, myself, Katie, Jordan, Wes, Kenny, Jeremy holding little Wesley, Jenell; Boys in front: Johnny, Andy, Paul

Katie and Jordan are currently very busy raising our two youngest grandchildren, Eden (six) and Philip (four). They are such precious little loves.

It is so wonderful now to be singing and playing instruments with my grandkids, who range from four to seventeen, and especially teaching them some of the same songs I sang to Jeremy and Joel as babies and small boys.

Jordan and Katie

Eden and Philip,
first day of kindergarten and preschool

Wes and I continue to travel to Millstadt, Illinois, to visit his family. It's always fun seeing them, and his mom is such a great host. We love playing games after eating. We went out two years ago for Pat's eighty-fifth birthday and had a wonderful dinner and reunion at the senior center in Millstadt.

I recently found a picture of our parents together in front of our second home, which we lived in for twenty-five years and where we raised our kids in Spokane, Washington, and made most of our family memories. It also includes Mark's parents who continued to stay in touch and join us at Christmas, birthdays, and events after Wes and I got married. Ben and Helen came to our first house for Christmas. Kenny commented to one of his friends when he was in elementary school, preparing for a grandparents' day event at his school, "I have three sets of grandparents!" His classmate didn't believe him. But that is how close Ben and Helen were to us and the kids. Things healed more through the years when we could be together after Mark wasn't controlling our relationship.

Left to right: Wally, Pat, Helen, Ben, Lois, Hank with me and Wes in front

On Kauai, where Bali Ha'i was filmed for South Pacific

Wes and I were also able to go back to Hawaii but not Maui (yet!). We were able to visit Bali Ha'i, Makana Mountain in Kauai. The movie *South Pacific* was filmed in this area, and it was so much fun to be there together.

You read earlier about that special guitar Cliff gave to me. What's really neat is that, to this day, that same guitar still works well and rarely needs tuning. When it is tuned, it holds for a very long time. I've used that guitar for more than thirty years of teaching to lead students during classes and assemblies in private and public schools. I also played it recently to record "Yield."

The redemptive part of this includes not just my life and our lives but Mark's life. He is seventy-five now and continues to live in a group home outside of Spokane. Jeremy and Joel have been in touch with him at times. I was amazed that he came to both of their weddings and seemed to be doing better since he was taking his meds. The guardian made sure he made it to both weddings dressed up in a suit!

Mark shakes a lot with tremors. It may be from the medications he's taking, but he is now pleasant, not at all like he was in the past. Wes and I have talked on the phone with him. I actually visited him a couple of times this year with my very close friend, Sherrell, who was my neighbor in Spokane for twenty-five years. Mark always has a song to share with us. Isn't that a switch! From a man who was obsessed with telling me that I put music above God as an idol and that I couldn't play piano and sing to now singing daily himself! He says he prays for all of us, too, and he is clearer in his mind than I've seen in a long time and has a sweet spirit about him. It's been a process to forgive him, but I know I have. I'm free and I hope he is. He seems to be. Jeremy and I went to show him his grandchildren when Ellie was a baby. He was overjoyed that we came for the visit before they headed back to Africa.

The owner of the group home walked me out recently, asking how the visit went.

I said, "He seems like he's doing well. We even sang together. Can I ask, is he taking meds?"

"Oh yes. I check people's backgrounds well before accepting them." He said a few more things that confirmed it was wise to leave Mark when I did. I feel he is getting the best care possible and in a safe place. It's still hard to see his physical condition. His feet are red and calloused. He's bent over when he walks. He seems about half the size he was even three to four years ago. I have to say, I still felt like a visiting nurse or caring friend when I saw him recently. All the old feelings of hurt are now diminished. I forgive him totally and feel removed from all that past. It's been *redeemed!*

Mark meets Elisabeth Joy!

Joy has truly come in this new morning … "He who did not spare his own Son, but gave him up for us all—how will he not also, along with him, graciously give us all things?" (Romans 8:32).

My very favorite Scripture is Isaiah 41:10–13, and it says:

> So do not fear, for I am with you; do not be dismayed, for I am your God. I will strengthen you and help you; I will uphold you with my righteous right hand.
>
> All who rage against you will surely be ashamed and disgraced; those who oppose you will be as nothing and perish. Though you search for your enemies, you will not find them. Those who wage war against you will be as nothing at all. For I am the LORD your God who takes hold of your right hand and says to you, Do not fear; I will help you.

The phrase *right hand* is used here in two different ways. In verse 10, He upholds me with *His* right hand, and in verse 13, He takes hold of *my* right hand. He is God, and I know He upholds us and protects us, and it makes me realize again how personal He is when it says He holds *my* right hand. It reminds me of my earlier days of walking home for lunch in second grade, alone but feeling like Jesus was holding my hand.

In Mark 16:19, it says, "After the Lord Jesus had spoken to them, he was taken up into heaven and he sat at the right hand of God." As I've pondered this over the years, I've thought, *How can the Lord hold me by my right hand if He sits on the right hand of the Father?* The answer came as a comforting revelation, and it's been such a security for my own heart—*I am in the middle of the Father and Jesus.* The Father, me, Jesus. He is at the right hand of the Father but also can hold *my* right hand if I'm in between them. And the Holy Spirit is in me. The Trinity! How comforting! Of course, this is in the spirit realm. But we can have that comfort here on earth!

We all can be in that place.

Psalm 31:12–16 says,

> I am forgotten as though I were dead; I have become like broken pottery. For I hear many whispering, "Terror on every side!" They conspire against me and plot to take my life. But I trust in you, Lord; I say, "You are my God." My times are in your hands; deliver me from the hands of my enemies, from those who pursue me. Let your face shine on your servant; save me in your *unfailing love.*

He has delivered me! And continues to. I've discovered a new meaning of the phrase "being used," and it's a *good* thing when you're in the hands of the Potter. He's taken my broken and shattered pot and reformed it into a new one. In the Old Testament, Jeremiah 18:3–4 says, "I went down to the potter's house, and I saw him working at the wheel. But the pot he was shaping from the clay was marred in his hands; so the potter formed it into another pot, shaping it as seemed best to him."

I'm so glad He hasn't given up on me but continues to mold and shape me according to what *He* sees best, and all I must do is yield and allow Him to have his perfect way.

Help me hear You every day, Lord, saying, "This is the way; walk in it" (Isaiah 30:21).

And that's also my hope for you, dear reader.

To God be all the glory! He's such a good, good Father who loves us all, no matter what.

May you be set free to fly!

Drawn by Eden Rose (my six-year-old granddaughter), on Jan.25, 2024

ORDER INFORMATION

Additional copies of this book can be ordered
wherever Christian books are sold.